PRAISE

"In this book, a master of optimal performance becomes a student of optimal performance. If you want to understand and create excellence in a human collective, this volume is a precious gift. Cherish it, and it will take you where conventional minds cannot go."

—**Professor Robert E. Quinn** | Center for Positive Organizations, University of Michigan

"Very few senior business executives are as well-read, familiar with rigorous research, and actively applying validated principles of leadership as David Drews. His book doubles your money—it provides a rich summary of empirically validated principles molded into an easily understood and remembered framework, and it offers practical illustrations and stories of incredible success achieved by an extraordinary executive. This is a unique book that will enrich and enlighten anyone wanting to achieve excellence for themselves and for their organization."

—**Kim Cameron** | William Russell Kelly Professor Emeritus of Management & Organizations, Stephen M. Ross School of Business, and Professor Emeritus of Higher Education, School of Education, University of Michigan

"*Teamflow* is a book designed for all leaders interested in bringing their team and organization to an optimal level of performance. David Drews weaves together a comprehensive set of studies and examples to provide an inspiring guide to creating teamflow in any situation. The book develops a compelling and easy-to-understand IMPACT framework as a guide to developing teamflow. *Teamflow* provides valuable lessons at a time when leaders need inspiration and insightful guidance about how to lead to bring forth sustainable excellence and the best of humanity. *Teamflow* is an excellent read that will excite and empower you to unlock potential, capacity, and strength in your organization."

—**Jane Dutton** | Founder, Positive Organizational Scholarship

"Drews does the seemingly impossible. He pulls together the various components of Positive Organizational Scholarship into a model of Teamflow. Weaving his personal stories with a myriad of research findings, he provides an accessible way for all of us to deepen our IMPACT in our own lives, our organizations, and those most important to us."

—**Gretchen Spreitzer** | Associate Dean, Engaged Learning and Professional Development, Keith E. and Valerie J. Alessi Professor of Business Administration, Stephen M. Ross School of Business, University of Michigan

"In this timely and well-researched book, David Drews provides a clear roadmap to combining values, meaning, and those we care about to create a thriving organization. His clear framework, empirical evidence, and decades of experience inform a perspective that most of us are in desperate need of during these challenging times. As physical and emotional distances continue to widen through a global pandemic, the national polity continues to polarize, and the gig economy threatens conventional definitions of work and worker, David's IMPACT approach reminds us that we all have it in us to return to a state of teamflow."

—**Julia Lee Cunningham** | Associate Professor of Management & Organizations, Faculty Co-Director, Center for Positive Organizations Stephen M. Ross School of Business, University of Michigan

"David Drews' Teamflow is a treasure trove of important thoughts on how to excel when working as teams and in teams. Describing the mix of factors that come together as Teamflow, the book captures both the richness and simplicity of meaningful collaborative work. The theoretical concepts and stories presented in the book draw richly from the cutting-edge academic research, business world, and David's personal experiences; they take the reader to an exciting journey on a positive psychology of teams."

—**Mari Kira, PhD** | Assistant Professor of Psychology, Department of Psychology, Univesity of Michigan

"David Drews is an outstanding transformational leader who has significantly helped others better understand the elements of 'Teamwork' and how the 'IMPACT Model' can generate optimized performance. Realizing how mistakes create opportunities for learning is a great step towards achieving positive teamflow that is so eloquently stated in this fantastic book. You will truly enjoy reading and applying the principles from *Teamflow* and it will provide you with an opportunity to learn from the very best."

—**Lenora Hardy-Foster** | President and CEO, Judson Center

"At the Center for Positive Organizations we talk about bringing out the best in people leading to high organizational performance. *Teamflow* offers a concrete guide for how to do this in a memorable framework. It moves from mindset and character into the elements required for collaborative action that creates lasting, meaningful change and positive impact."

—**Esther Kyte** | Managing Director, Center for Positive Organizations, Stephen M. Ross School of Business, University of Michigan

"Drews helps us appreciate that a positive mindset matters . . . immensely. By artfully distilling some of the best academic research, along with a "here's how to put it into action" approach, *Teamflow* reveals both the science and practical implication of positive practices. It's a must-read for those looking to take control of their business and personal lives."

—**Jim Mallozzi** | Principal, Mindset Advisors, LLC

"*Teamflow* is a fascinating read with IMPACT! I found it uplifting as I read page after page. Filled with David's personal experiences and countless referenced examples that provide more understanding for "Inspiring Positive Change and Purpose," *Teamflow* is refreshing and inspiring: in stark contrast to the continuous negativity of the current news cycles and across our political spectrum. I find application in my business, personal, and family life. Positive IMPACT is a system that leads to continuous harmony and Teamflow."

—**Roy Verstraete** | Founder, Private Directors Association, Detroit Chapter; board member of companies in the US, Europe, Latin America and Canada; former president and CEO, Anchor Danly Corp.

"David shares a compelling case for employing Positive Organizational Scholarship to shift from old ways of thinking to generative new ways of doing. A valuable resource for anyone looking to ignite engagement in their organization."

—**Betsy Erwin** | Co-Director, Engaged Learning and Innovation, Center for Positive Organizations

TEAMFLOW

The Science of Creating
Positive Leadership
Practices with IMPACT

DAVID DREWS

Published in association with Per Capita Publishing, a division of Content Capital*.

ISBN 13: 978-1-954020-22-1 (Paperback)
ISBN 13: 978-1-954020-49-8 (Hardback)
ISBN 13: 978-1-954020-23-8 (Ebook)

Library of Congress Cataloging-in-Publication Data
Names: Drews, David W., author.
Title: Teamflow / David W. Drews
Description: First Edition | Texas: Per Capita Publishing (2022)
Identifiers: LCCN 2022902291 (print)

14 15 16 17 18 19 10 9 8 7 6 5 4 3 2 1

First Edition

For Lisa, the most positive person I know!

CONTENTS

FOREWORD

In twenty years of serving as faculty director or core faculty member of the Center for Positive Organizations (CPO) at the University of Michigan Ross School of Business, I've met many business executives who dream of writing a book one day. Few realize their dream. Of those who do, even fewer are able to combine decades of business and leadership experience with a deep knowledge of the scientific research on positive leadership and organizations. That's what David Drews has accomplished in *Teamflow*.

I first met Dave in May 2016, when he became an executive in residence at CPO, joining a small, august group of retired CEOs and senior executives who have concluded extraordinarily successful careers and come to CPO to offer their knowledge, experience, and wisdom to our students, researchers, members of our Positive Organizations Consortium, and more. Dave was executive vice president, chief financial officer, and executive committee member of an international marketing agency where he and the top team grew a small firm into a global company with more than forty offices. Among many achievements, Dave led acquisitions and helped launch greenfield operations throughout the US, Europe, and Asia. In short, Dave brought a wealth of practical business experience to CPO.

My first impression of Dave was his passion for learning. Right after joining CPO, he asked for a summary of the field of Positive Organizational Scholarship or POS—the scientific foundation of positive cultures, leadership, and organizations. We provided a copy of *The Oxford Handbook of Positive Organizational Scholarship*—a "summary" that clocks in at more than 1,000 pages. And yet he devoured it, taking hundreds and hundreds of notes. He followed references to read the primary sources on which the summary was based. And he searched for and documented many examples and stories of the positive principles and practices he was reading about. Dave's six-year journey culminates in this book.

Teamflow is organized around an easy-to-remember acronym: IMPACT. *I* is for identification, which requires you to look inside and take inventory: What are your core values, your guiding principles? What are your signature strengths? The second letter, *M*, is for meaning. This is your mission in life, your fundamental purpose, and your positive vision for yourself and your organization. *P* stands for perspective. This includes perspective-taking or the ability to see and appreciate the world from others' points of view. It also includes what we refer to in POS as "using a positive lens." This is the ability to see possibilities even in the most difficult and trying circumstances. *A*, for action, puts everything in motion by developing and implementing the how-to steps required to bring your purpose, mission, and vision into reality. Of course, little happens without *C*, collaboration, rallying others in support of the organization's vision and creating work environments in which people thrive.

Put all these elements together and you get *T*—teamflow—and superior performance as a result. I especially like the word teamflow. Until Dave coined it, English lacked a term that aptly summarized what happens when you fully live POS. Teamflow is part *chi*, the Chinese notion of the vital lifeforce or energy that animates all living things. Teamflow is part *flow*, a concept developed by psychologist Mihály Csíkszentmihályi to refer to a positive mental state of full engagement and complete absorption in an activity. Importantly, teamflow is a collective concept. It's an optimal state of experience and performance for individuals, teams, and organizations.

Teamflow will inspire you. It will provide you with new concepts, guiding principles, and proven practices that will help you become a better person and leader. It will help you find joy at work. It will be a reference that you will return to again and again on your journey to live a full life, live your mission, and make a positive contribution to the world.

Wayne E. Baker
Robert P. Thome Professor of Business Administration and Faculty Co-Director, Center for Positive Organizations University of Michigan Stephen M. Ross School of Business Author of *All You Have to Do Is Ask* (2020)

PROLOGUE

It is easy to see the glass half empty rather than half full. Our minds scan for danger. During unprecedented times, we look for positive threads we can weave into our approach to daily life. The pandemic that started in 2020 will leave its mark on history; how we persevered and overcame adversity will be memorable. No time is more important than the present to embrace the science of optimizing our performance and the performance of those around us. We want to create positive spirals that can be replicated. Fortunately, nearly twenty years of research exists in the body of knowledge called Positive Organizational Scholarship, and it provides a formula for success in both flourishing and challenging times.

I grew up in a small town in Western Michigan. My parents and grandparents did not have the benefit of a four-year college degree. They worked hard, provided for us, and instilled a clear moral compass. I recognized in high school that to achieve what I sought to achieve in life, I needed to pay very close attention to others and what made them successful. Through college and my career, I made note of these attributes and mirrored the best of the practices I observed. It became part of the fabric of which I am sewn. I saw first-hand the benefits of embodying the principles outlined in the pages that follow.

My career led me from that small town to the C-Suite, into boardrooms, and onto a team that took a small business and grew it through green-field start-ups, acquisitions, joint ventures, and organic growth into a worldwide organization with thousands of employees. Without realizing the formal body of research was being established simultaneously, I clung to the threads of Positive Organizational Scholarship.

Having consciously practiced Positive Organizational Scholarship for more than thirty-five years, I am captivated by the work of world-class scholars proving the attributes that drive optimal performance—positive deviance, in the parlance of Positive Organizational Scholarship—reading book after book on the topic. Aren't we all interested in optimizing our performance and that of those around us? Focusing on this causes each of us to assess and reassess what we are doing that contributes to peak performance. When we achieve it, it is a beautiful feeling, like hitting the sweet spot on a golf club. We don't just know it. We feel it. It makes us want to do it over and over again.

But like golf, it isn't easy to do and is hard to replicate. Each circumstance is different. Each requires a unique solution. Is there a way to consistently break down the process and improve the odds of optimizing performance—causing flourishing in individuals, groups, and society? The answer lies in the sum of Positive Organizational Scholarship research. This research gives us a way to replicate positive change and teach it to others.

The span of topics covered in the following pages is vast, collected by more than five hundred researchers and scholars, and each point is a thread of understanding. These threads help us understand what motivates us and those around us. They provide a framework for leading by example, both personally and professionally. The threads of Positive Organizational Scholarship weave together into a rope we can hold onto in both good times and bad, helping us overcome obstacles.

Over the past six years, the following concepts have helped me overcome the challenges I've faced. The research has helped ground my thoughts and provide insight for consideration, prompting solutions that I otherwise might not have considered.

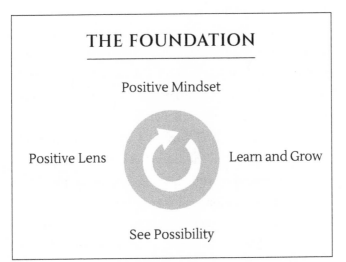

THE FOUNDATION

Positive Mindset

Positive Lens   Learn and Grow

See Possibility

As I searched for a single word that describes the science scholars call Positive Organizational Scholarship, I came up empty. "Teamwork" did not adequately address optimizing performance. At its root, teamwork is based on work. When we excel, the effort of work eases and disappears into the background. We experience flow. We become so immersed in what we are doing, the concept of time is lost; concentration is heightened, and we are fully in touch with our senses and those around us. We reach a different level—an optimized state.[1] "Teamflow" describes optimizing the performance of a group, allowing individuals AND the group to excel. Knowing the components of Teamflow can allow us to experience it more often.

In the text that follows, I've abbreviated key tenets, shared stories, and applied research in a way that, hopefully, makes it understandable and actionable. If we create a path toward practical application, more of us will benefit from the human science principles behind optimizing performance.

Positive Organizational Scholarship is world-class research; it is proven with validated empirical evidence. It works. It looks not just at positive outliers, but is grounded in research that fully evaluates the effects that drive positive deviance—behavior that far and away exceeds normal operating behavior. And, because it is based on principles researched by scholars, the results are based on original theories and validated with rigorous, systematic procedures using careful definitions and peer review.

Optimized performance is hard to achieve. That said, haven't we all been "in the zone" at some point? It could have been in sports, business, school, a club, a volunteer activity, or some other aspect of our lives. The zone we all seek maximizes our potential. It makes us feel good. It is infectious. It helps those around us—elevating their performance as well.

The principles of Positive Organizational Scholarship are practiced around us, and often we don't even realize it. When I was young, I spent virtually every Saturday morning in a fishing boat with my uncle. I cannot recall the details of a single conversation, but somehow, I seem to recall everything he said. It is captured in Teamflow. He innately understood and practiced it. Modeling words and actions is a powerful combination that accelerates the learning of others.

The Positive IMPACT process systematically links the concepts of Positive Organizational Scholarship. When we have conceptual order, recall improves substantially. This allows replication of results and improvement, highlighting a path that capitalizes on intrinsic motivation and allows us to achieve a state of flow more frequently. It provides self-assurance. When we look at problems as challenges, we more readily resolve them. And, practically speaking, having a series of concrete actions provides a roadmap to consider and adapt to each situation.

Complex problems are easier to solve by breaking them into much smaller problems. Couldn't we apply this problem-solving method to the science of optimizing performance? We could then apply the methodology to personal and professional challenges at both the macro and micro levels. The goal of Positive IMPACT is to make the complex, simple.

The nature of scholarly research is to focus on specific areas and deeply analyze specific topics. Then, pulling together specific elements and sequencing them into a map—a map that simplifies and organizes the research—allows us to stitch together a methodology that moves us toward optimizing performance. Hopefully, we can positively IMPACT performance, ultimately creating Teamflow in a way that moves forward and creates a contagion, simultaneously improving our lives and the lives of those around us.

IMPACT represents an acronym for the process:

- Identification
- Meaning
- Perspective
- Action
- Collaboration
- Teamflow

The first step is *Identification*. We need to understand what makes us tick. How can we become our best selves? Who are we, and what do we believe in? Will we stand up to our values in the heat of the moment, when times are tough and others may be weakening? We need to have our internal priorities in order and identify the challenges we are looking to solve, along with the desired result.

The next tenet is *Meaning*. Meaning combines our personal purpose, the purpose of colleagues, and the group's purpose. How do we find alignment in each of these points of view? If we can find a way to adopt a common purpose—ideally sharing ownership of that purpose—many obstacles faced will more easily be overcome.

We need *Perspective*. We need to look at everything from other points of view. Who will be affected? Will it be a positive or negative impact for them? Will anyone or any group stand in the way? How do we create a solution that brings everyone on board? All those affected need to be considered. Their point of view needs to be valued and included.

The more complex the goal, the more detailed the *Action* plan should be.[2] Specific steps need to be taken to gain momentum, and diversity of perspectives and background can aid in solving complex goals.[3] When making progress, initialization is often followed by uncertainty, which can lead to transformation, which can then be followed by routinization. Often, an unexpected change happens and the process may start all over again. Every situation, even if similar to past situations, needs a bespoke, unique solution. We need to constantly reevaluate and improve.[4]

Nothing happens without *Collaboration*. Trust must exist to facilitate change. High quality connections and relationships are key.[5] Change requires listening, patience, adaptability, and respect—respecting others' points of views when they are different from our own. My father always said one of the most important things in life is getting along with others; we naturally want to help those that help us, are kind to us, listen to us, or provide us insight.

Weaving together *Action* and *Collaboration* is critical. This is an interactive process—one informs the other. Listening for clues on resistance creates awareness and adapts our plans. Through high quality relationships, insights come over conversations at meals, brief chats, or in discussions that address other topics—literally anytime or anywhere we are with others. Feedback loops assess success and improvement follows. It needs to be transparent and needs to create learning. Success, as it occurs, needs to be amplified.

Ultimately, the sum of each of the previous elements form Teamflow. Based on the concept of *chi*, also known as "flow," the team unifies in a way that far exceeds teamwork.[6] The best groups flow seamlessly together. They unify behind a goal and think beyond themselves. They achieve a point of positive deviance, as the scholars call it; a sustained state of exceptional performance far above the norm. This is what we seek.

Inasmuch as these steps sound sequential, that is not the case. Each step informs the others. Modifications are constant, but the IMPACT framework places the steps in logical pieces that can be analyzed. It points out gaps that should have been considered or that would improve the probability of success. McKinsey, a consulting firm, states that nearly 70 percent of organizational change fails.[7] Certainly, much room for improvement exists, and improvement is more likely with the science behind IMPACT.

Most times, the progress we are trying to make is complex and dynamic. This requires fluid thought and adaptation. Each step needs to be revisited and adjusted.

Only through free-flowing iterations of the IMPACT model can complex solutions be found. When altering one aspect, other aspects should be reconsidered to determine if adjustment is needed. Honing the solution takes time, resolve, and patience. It takes a willingness to change and, in some cases, letting go of ownership if someone else can more quickly attain a goal with our support.

As we make progress, it is helpful to map ideas first and write the details afterward.[8] Capturing key words that allow us to brainstorm solutions across the full IMPACT spectrum improves solution development speeds. Limitations of singular analytical thinking can be supplemented by our creative capacity.

As ideas develop, we can expect resistance. Bob Quinn, a scholar and founder of Positive Organizational Scholarship at the University of Michigan, has seen the sequence of "laugh, argue, and attack with anger or threats" from those affected by change.[9] Some look to discourage us with a series of tactics. The key is perseverance. If we believe in what we are seeking, we should consider a new approach. Revisit each of the steps. We need to look for impediments that prevent the solution and press onward. Resistance is better than apathy, passive-aggressive behavior, or no feedback at all. We can almost always learn something from resistance and increase our chance of success as we adopt new thinking strategies.[10]

Small changes can have outsized results. Consider the difference between water at 211 degrees and 212 degrees

Fahrenheit. Water at 211 degrees is just very, very hot water. At the boiling temperature of 212 degrees, steam is created. Steam can power a locomotive. It can move a ship. Positive movement can happen from an incredibly small change.

"Small wins are a steady application of a small advantage" wrote Karl Wieck, an organizational theorist at the University of Michigan. Small wins build upon themselves. They create a culture that expects to win and looks for every advantage, large and small. Small wins should be celebrated, as they lead to progress. Incremental advantage powers success. The momentum of small wins creates the opportunity for differentiation that leads to large wins.[11]

> Small changes can have outsized results.

The impact of small wins can be surprising. Let's say we started measuring strength at the start of a year-long fitness program and that our strength began at a score of 250. Over the course of the year, we worked out an average of three times per week, gaining an almost imperceptible one to two strength points each time—literally less than 1 percent. At the end of the twelve-months, we look back and realize the cumulative effect of those workouts led to more than doubling our strength score to 525. Electronic resistance weight machines measure exactly this. I have seen this first-hand.

We often are not able or fail to measure small changes. They happen in all aspects of our lives—education, diet, fitness, organizational improvement, skill development, teamwork, and more. Small wins matter, adding up to big wins.

Knowing the difference between good and great can be measured in microns and impacts our approach through Positive Organizational Scholarship, or Teamflow. We need a positive lens, a growth mindset, and to recognize and embrace possibility.

To quote Jocko Willink and Leif Babin, authors of the book *Extreme Ownership: How U.S. Navy Seals Lead and Win*:

When ego clouds our judgment and prevents us from
seeing the world as it is, then ego becomes destructive. A
leader . . . does not take credit for his or her team's success but bestows that honor upon his subordinate leaders
and team members. The leader's attitude sets the tone
for the entire team. Acknowledge mistakes and admit
failure, take ownership of them and develop a plan to
win . . . A leader has nothing to prove, but everything
to prove. The only meaningful measure for a leader is
whether the team succeeds or fails. Outcomes are never
certain; success never guaranteed.[12]

The leadership principles in Willink and Babin's book
are complemented and supplemented through the work of
world-class researchers who look to provide a clear signal
toward optimizing performance, cutting out the noise. That
signal, based on research results that can be replicated, is
what Teamflow and Positive Organizational Scholarship are
all about. It builds on and complements research by both
Amy Edmondson of Harvard on the principles of successful
teams and the principles of flow proposed by Mihály Csíkszentmihályi at Claremont Graduate University.

At times during the COVID-19 pandemic, we may have
begun to wonder whether these principles are theoretical
or practical. We have seen the best and worst of character
in the pandemic, and individualism runs counter to optimizing performance. When we see selfish behavior, it drains

our energy. Individualism can lead to personal validation rather than considering what actually is right. Alternatively, openness, learning, thinking about the perspective of others, compassion, and empathy will lift us up. When we see it displayed in others, it energizes us. We are drawn to those who radiate incredible character and bring out the best in us. We are part of a larger system—a system in which we can thrive together. We can and will succeed, even when significant challenges arise and persist.

Books on leadership have been written time and again based on experience and provide valuable insight based on perspective. This book differs in that it centers on the research, then includes personal experience and perspective that aligns with that research. The work being advanced by the Center for Positive Organizations at the University of Michigan and the scholars who are building this body of research base their work on theories that can be tested and results that can be replicated. The scientific foundation is real. The results are impactful.

We all altered aspects of our lives during the pandemic in some way. Of the many changes I have made, one small change is analogous to the impact of Teamflow: like many others, I started making bread. Though I knew nothing about bread making, I started experimenting (it helped having a great friend who coached me). The fact that something as seemingly inert as yeast is activated with warm water, causing flour to rise, doubling in size, amazed me. The same thing happens when we practice the research shared in this book. Those around us rise up. We each grow.

Getting to the top of a pyramid—Everest performance: the best of what a group can be—rests on peak human performance.[13] We have all seen it time and again: a group with great talent and leadership develops tremendous momentum and achieves extraordinary results. The group co-creates energy. It has a gravitational pull to all those exposed to it. People want to be a part of it. People feed off the energy of the group. It creates zest, makes us feel alive.[14]

When alignment exists, a group flows. When individuals adopt the goals of the group as their own goals, mountains can be moved. As Shawn Achor, author of the foreword in *How to Be a Positive Leader*, has said: "The greatest competitive advantage in the modern economy is a positive and engaged brain."[15] Dutton and Spreitzer, in *How to Be a Positive Leader*, call the state of optimizing performance above the norm the "zone of possibility"—a zone that raises performance from current levels to the best it can be.[16]

Positive Organizational Scholarship helps us understand explicitly what we know implicitly, giving us a framework to understand and improve upon the natural instincts that drive optimal performance.

Teamflow is at once a paradox of being incredibly simple—treating people in a way that draws out the best in them—and incredibly complex—determining the common factors that underlie performance and modulating these factors to lift a specific individual or team.

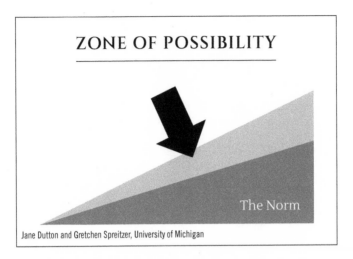

Jane E Dutton and Gretchen Spreitzer, adapted from *How to Be a Positive Leader: Insights from Leading Thinkers on Positive Organizations*

Each step along the way feels like a multiplication formula. That is, if anything clearly fails (is a zero) the implemented changes stop and we revert to the norm. This does not mean we accept the norm—quite the opposite. Optimized performance has been done and continues to be done. If we want extraordinary performance, we need to pursue it, day in and day out. We need to reassess, change, and continuously improve. One step at a time can make progress and drive change.

Achieving Teamflow is fun—yes, fun. Seeing the impact of that change in ourselves and those around us provides great personal satisfaction. Aligning the goal with our personal purpose fuels passion and provides fulfillment. Isn't that what we are all after?

Chapter 1

POSITIVE FRAMING

"A negative thought never leads to a positive result."
—Bob Tewksbury, *Ninety Percent Mental*[17]

Mindset matters. Remarkable differences exist in the way we frame our thoughts. Are we looking at issues as challenges or as problems? Are we looking at possibilities or limitations? Are we open to new thought or do we have a fixed mindset, and are the words we use reflective of our mindset? Are we drawing out the best in others? Success hinges on a positive attitude. Study after study show the dramatic impact of a positive mindset. Positive spirals are infectious; small wins become big wins. Controlling our mindset is our starting point.[18]

Research psychologist Sonja Lyubomirsky has found that generosity, kindness, gratitude, and reframing situations with a positive lens also raises our level of happiness.

Why is a positive outlook so hard to maintain? For starters, negative input triggers our flight or fight response. As Lyubomirsky states: "Our brains evolved to focus on the negative, because it is the most effective way to learn."[19] Negative input outweighs positive input by a factor of between two and five to one. Said a different way, a general rule is that it takes four positive comments to neutralize each negative comment. When we receive multiple positive comments for each negative comment, it moves us toward optimizing performance.

De-energizing relationships have more effect than positive relationships. Our brains are wired to scan for danger, so we magnify the negative. If we consciously look for the positive in all that we do, we can offset the power of negativity.[20] That said, if we get to a positive to negative ratio of eight to one or higher, we begin to feel as though we are losing sight of reality.[21] As Kim Cameron, a pioneer and cofounder of Positive Organizational Scholarship says, "All sunshine causes a desert."[22] We need a healthy balance of positive factors in our life—ideally a ratio of at least two to one, but not greater than eight to one—in order to fuel optimal performance.

> If we consciously look for the positive in all that we do, we can offset the power of negativity.

Research shows the power of negative to be two to five times the power of positive experiences. Non-emotional negative effects, like the loss of money, tend toward the lower end of the spectrum. In these cases, the rational part of the brain can help offset negativity. When emotions are involved, the number of positive experiences needs to rise to three to five times the number of negative experiences to get us to our optimal state. A positive mindset is essential.[23]

Whenever I have a challenge that is extremely hard to solve, I work from home. It gives me time to focus on pulling the problem apart and taking a pass at resolutions. As part of this ritual, I put on an old sweatshirt—my original "Michigan" sweatshirt—from my MBA days. I want to feel smart. I want to be my best.

What I did not know until recently is that it actually works. In the same way a great coach fires up their team with positive imagery, putting ourselves in a positive frame of mind improves performance and allows access to our best selves. Psychologist John Bargh calls this "priming the adaptive subconscious." We achieve things that we otherwise may not have considered possible.[24]

This positive flow, *chi*, is what we are looking for—the state of mind when things flow naturally, when answers jump out at us. We begin piggybacking ideas off one another to reach better solutions.

Why is it that I felt better wearing that ratty old University of Michigan sweatshirt? Or that I always play a better round of golf after replaying a positive memory in my mind on my way to the course?

As it turns out, science has the answers. Two Dutch researchers conducted a study where participants were asked to imagine life as a professor. They performed significantly better in answering Trivial Pursuit questions than those who imagined themselves as soccer hooligans. The "professor" participants answered 56 percent of the questions correctly, while the "soccer hooligans" only answered 43 percent correctly. The talent pools were the same, but the mentality of being "smart" actually made the first group perform better.[25] Testing has been duplicated with other groups, such as minorities. In one such study performed by Claude Steele and Joshua Aronson, correct answers were cut in half due to perceived differences held by the respondents. Priming matters.[26]

High school and college students have gone through similar research exercises. The results are the same, repeatedly. Positive framing markedly improves performance in retaining words learned in a foreign language or correctly answering questions on standardized tests.

Getting ourselves in a positive frame of mind makes a difference. It is the first step. We need to be our best. It improves our performance, lowers stress, and improves sleep.[27] Positive framing makes us feel good. It is not only a great way to start; it is the right way to prepare oneself for any challenge.

I enjoy golf (when I am not shanking the ball into the woods). Golf is a tough sport. When we misfire, it can stay with us. It can affect our consciousness, our mindset.

In April 2016, Jordan Spieth was leading the Masters by five strokes going into the last round. After bogeying the 10th and 11th hole, he quadruple-bogeyed the 12th. His swing malfunctioned. He left two shots short—in the water. He lost by three strokes.[28]

In 2017, fate struck again. Leading on the final day of the British Open, he hit his tee shot on the 13th far to the right, over large mounds, and nearly onto the driving range. Frankly, it was a shot any of us could have hit. It was that bad. It took twenty minutes to assess the situation. He had an unplayable lie. He could not see the green. He dropped the ball on the driving range and had his caddy watch from the top of the hill as he struck the ball.

His shot cleared the mounds and ended just short of the green. With a chip shot and a putt, he bogeyed the hole. Amazing. The shot kept him in contention to win.

His caddy, a former math teacher, told Jordan the tide had turned. This was his time to excel. And excel he did. He finished five shots under par on the final five holes, winning the tournament. His caddy knew about positive framing and put it to use in real time.[29]

Not only did Spieth win, but he also exemplified positive behavior, expressing gratitude for the patience of his playing partner, Matt Kuchar, who waited without complaint as Spieth worked out his options for properly playing the hole. Positive framing runs the gamut of all that we do in life.

Once, I took a golf lesson focused on putting. The instructor told the story of a friend who was a tour pro. He had just finished a round at a professional golf event. Over dinner, the pro commented he was the best putter on the PGA Tour. Everyone paused, and the tour pro was asked for clarity, given that he did not even rank in the top 100 for putting skill. The pro simply said, "Only I need to believe

I am the best." We need the same mindset in each of us. Without positive belief, we cannot achieve our best.

Thirty years ago, major league baseball players would never have considered the need for a mental skills coach. Now, team after team engages in positive framing. Mental skill performance coaches teach players to identify negative thoughts, delete them, and replace them with positive thoughts by repeating anchor statements.

Anchor statements are positive, affirming phrases that reinforce the positive mindset of the player. As Bob Tewksbury, former All-Star pitcher and now mental skills coach says, "A negative thought never leads to a positive result."[30]

This applies to each of us, and at early ages in our development too. Just before having four-year-olds perform an activity with blocks, researchers prompted one set of children with thirty seconds of a positive memory, another set with thirty seconds of a negative memory, and left a third group unprompted, as a control group. Remarkably, those prompted with positive memories performed 50 percent faster and more accurately than those prompted with negative memories, and 30 percent better than the control group.[31]

> As Bob Tewksbury, former All-Star pitcher and now mental skills coach says, "A negative thought never leads to a positive result."

Cornell University repeated a similar test with emergency room doctors. ER doctors prompted with positive emotions properly diagnosed patients 20 percent more quickly and accurately than their unprompted colleagues.[32]

A positive mindset matters. It improves performance.

Positive framing raises resilience, raises memory retention, and creates better relationships. "Positive emotions broaden our thinking and behavior through making us more creative, integrative, flexible, open to information, efficient, and open to others, among other benefits . . . [persons experiencing positive emotions] regulate negative emotional experiences, have close relationships, buffer depressive symptoms, and recover better from the stressors of daily life."[33] Getting the mind ready increases the possibility of each of us achieving our best selves. It opens our minds to possibility.

We each need to recall memories of when we performed at our best; think of the time, the place, who we were with, and any other details we can recall. These memories allow us to replicate the positive energy that allowed us to excel.

In the end, we need to work to retain great memories over time. Chris Peterson of the University of Michigan found that the more we can identify what makes us feel good, the more we are able to replicate that feeling of happiness. We need to consciously seek to retain and recall positive emotions to regenerate the cycle of positive experience and move ourselves into a positive frame of mind to improve our lives and the lives of those around us.[34]

We also need to know our strengths. Eighty percent of employees do not feel they use their strengths every day. Use of strengths lowers turnover and stress while raising productivity, problem solving ability, teamwork, energy, wellbeing, and the immune system.[35] Research shows using our strengths raises productivity by 8 percent.[36]

A study in New Zealand found that those of us who know our strengths are nine times more likely to be thriving. Additionally, we are eighteen times more likely to thrive if we use those strengths. When we know our strengths, we feel good about them—positive framing—and use them more often. Strengths allow us to achieve a state of flow more often.[37]

> Strengths allow us to achieve a state of flow more often.

Simon Sinek, in his book, *Leaders Eat Last*, outlines an understanding of the four primary chemicals in our brain that drive behavior and enhance our feelings of accomplishment, trust, and community.

Endorphins and dopamine exist so that we can set and accomplish goals. Endorphins mask pain. They provide an incentive, a boost, to keep us going in response not only to exercise, but also to fear and stress. Endorphins are also released during laughter—which explains why a light-hearted moment can ease the stress of a difficult situation.

Dopamine is released when we accomplish a goal or cross milestones toward a goal. As a "To Do" list person, it is extremely satisfying when I cross off items that are finished. Dopamine keeps us focused. It guides us toward progress, rewarding us along the way. It creates a biological foundation behind hard work toward a difficult goal. Dopamine's downside can be addiction—drugs, alcohol, and electronic devices all set off a dopamine rush. We need to teach ourselves to delay gratification, reflecting on what is truly meaningful, rather than what generates a quick dopamine buzz.

Serotonin and oxytocin bridge the gap from individualistic thought to group dynamics:

> When we cooperate or look out for others, serotonin and oxytocin reward us with feelings of security, fulfillment, belonging, trust and camaraderie . . . And, when that happens, we find ourselves in the Circle of Safety, stress declines, fulfillment rises, our want to serve others increases and our willingness to trust others to watch our backs skyrockets. When these social incentives are inhibited, however, we become more selfish and more aggressive. Leadership falters. Cooperation declines. Stress increases as do paranoia and mistrust.[38]

Serotonin gives us a sense of pride. It gives us confidence that we are respected by others. It crosses boundaries and creates bonds between us. It rewards accomplishment that is shared, not individually owned. It is why parents feel proud of their children and why those very children give credit and thanks to their parents upon accomplishing goals.

> Trust is the backbone of empathy and cooperation.

Trust comes from oxytocin. Without oxytocin, everything breaks down. Trust is the backbone of empathy and cooperation. How could we have deep bonds with one another without trust? How could we accomplish our goals, at work or at home, if we did not trust others? "Oxytocin boosts our immune systems, makes us better problem solvers and makes us more resistant to the addictive qualities of dopamine."[39]

Deep inside our brains is the amygdala. The amygdala acts with alarm at any sign of danger. On the opposite side of the spectrum, the amygdala creates belonging cues if a person feels safe. We want strong social bonds. These bonds are enhanced neurologically when we are safe.[40]

When we are able to create emotion—activating the amygdala—we trigger a most powerful ally. Emotion is more powerful than rational thought. It drives us. It allows us to push onward in the face of challenges. Finding ways to activate emotion is key in making forward progress.[41]

> Emotion is more powerful than rational thought.

Knowing these factors—the amygdala, endorphins, dopamine, serotonin, and oxytocin—allows us to decode what makes us tick and guide ourselves into a positive mindset.

Brandeis University researchers found that our brains function differently when prompted with positive emotions. Using eye-tracking technology, researchers showed multiple pictures on slides to college students. Those prompted with positive emotions could recall pictures both in the center and the periphery of their vision. Those prompted with negative emotions generally only recalled the images in the center of their vision.

Our brains react differently when we have positive framing. The researchers theorize this difference may be attributed to our flight or fight response. We are able to relax and take in more information when positive rather than negative emotions are present.[42]

Here is a major take-away: We need to view all that we do in life as a learning experience. In sports, business, relationships, and every other aspect of our lives, we need to ask the question, "What could I do differently in the future that would improve the outcome?" Learning and growth are central themes that weave throughout the concepts of Teamflow.

The impact of a growth mindset has been studied by Carol Dweck, a researcher at Stanford University and author of *Mindset*. In her work, she creates distinction between a growth mindset and a fixed mindset. Her research shows that 40 percent of us have a fixed mindset, 40 percent have a growth mindset, and 20 percent are a blend.[43] Within these broad categories, each of us can vary and move between the growth and fixed mindsets. Specific circumstances or people can trigger movement toward a growth or fixed mindset.[44]

Believing we can learn and grow makes a huge difference. With a fixed mindset, we think our capabilities are already manifested and not influenced by our actions; it creates "a desire to look smart and therefore a tendency to avoid challenges, get defensive or give up easily, see effort as fruitless or worse, ignore useful negative feedback, feel

> We need to view all that we do in life as a learning experience.

threatened by the success of others," and achieve less than our full potential.[45] We fear being judged on outcomes, failure feels fatal, we micromanage, and we blame others.[46]

In contrast, a growth mindset is as it sounds: all about growing ourselves. It "leads to a desire to learn and therefore a tendency to embrace challenges, persist in the face of setbacks, seeing effort as the path to mastery, learn from criticism, find lessons and inspiration in the success of others," and therefore reach higher levels of achievement. We need to be grateful for every moment, every experience, and learn from it.[47] We cannot do it *yet*, but we are confident we will be able to do it eventually. We can achieve great things, and we will learn from failure as well as negative feedback. Our approach is to act, assess, and adjust with a constant eye toward learning and improving.[48]

When Roger Newton, the lead researcher on the team that created the statin drug Lipitor, was approached by the businesspeople in his organization, they expressed concern that he had failed four times. He corrected them by stating that his team had *learned* four times, and that had led to the development of the molecule that became Lipitor.

Each experience teaches us something—maybe something we did not want to know, but a learning nonetheless. As Newton says, there is a reason for the "re" in research. We must continuously retry many times as we search for progress.[49]

Ryan Quinn, a researcher at the University of Louisville, has studied learning from success and failure. He points out that success is less instructive than failure and can breed hubris, create biased learning, foster overconfidence, and hinder divergent thinking. Failure motivates learning. Success may not.[50]

We need to constructively anticipate failure, have situational awareness, push for diversity of thought, and be resilient. Imitating others through benchmarking decreases risk.[51]

After-action reviews can be great learning experiences, whether we seek to learn from a failure or look for elements that could have been improved inside of successes. Our mindset should be, "How do we do this even better?" We can always grow our capacity even when excellence is our starting point. Positive feedback tells us what to do, whereas negative feedback only tells us what not to do.

Lindy Greer, a researcher and faculty director of the Sanger Leadership Center at the University of Michigan, points out that after-action reviews are a great time to "leave the stripes at the door," allowing free exchange of information not hindered by rank or hierarchy. This is exactly the way the US Navy Seals conduct their after-action reviews.[52]

> Failure often follows success just as success often follows failure.

Failure often follows success just as success often follows failure. The key is continuous learning. We need to recombine our thoughts in new and different ways as well as redefine problems in constructive, positive ways.[53]

Positive Organizational Scholarship focuses on a learning mindset. Constant positive feedback is not what we are seeking; we need the balance and insight all feedback gives us. Processing information or passing along feedback in the most constructive way possible enables Teamflow. Often, we learn more from setbacks than we do from successes.

The impact of a positive mindset can take root in each of us.

Many of us cannot imagine the hardship of growing up as a poverty-stricken urban child and never having met your father; being expelled from school for pushing a teacher; seeing drugs packaged by one of the biggest drug dealers in the city—your mother; or having your uncle pick you up from middle school to tell you your mother had been murdered. The sum of such experiences is unimaginable.

Yet, in spite of experiencing all of that, Rob Murphy saw possibility and exemplified kindness, gratitude, and a positive mindset.

Murphy became the first in his family to graduate from college. He came home after college to teach and coach teams to the state basketball title, moving into the college ranks as an assistant coach at Kent State, then Syracuse—all the while staying positive.

He always looked forward. He always learned. He then became the head basketball coach at Eastern Michigan University, bringing life into a lifeless program. Now, he is the Senior Director of Player Personnel of the Detroit Pistons. Rob Murphy realized his purpose was to "help young men, many of whom grew up with challenges like me, realize they do not have to be products of their environment."[54]

His story, told in *Deep*, is a story of resilience, persistence, and determination. "Your mental makeup is what will separate you from others . . . change your mind[set] and you can change your entire life." Rob Murphy continues to reach higher, and he inspires others to make great impacts in their own lives.[55]

A positive frame of mind generates better outcomes. Positive framing is the precursor to achieving impact. It raises our confidence, our performance, and our results.[56]

> Positive framing is the precursor to achieving impact.

Self-confidence allows other-centricity. One must get beyond the "me" in order to achieve the best for "we." Confidence in our own ability, our own adaptability, and the collective knowledge of a group moves us to a higher state—a state of optimization.

None of this exists without a positive mindset. It all starts there. Creating a positive impact is not easy. It takes time. When we thrive, our performance markedly improves. We become more committed, proactive, and innovative. It permeates all aspects of our lives.[57] It is the starting point.

Chapter 2

IMPACT:
IDENTIFICATION

"Character, in the long run, is the decisive factor in
the life of an individual and of nations alike."
—Theodore Roosevelt[58]

What makes us tick? What motivates us? Our character and values are seen and influence those around
us. We need a clear view of who we are and what we are
seeking. We need to find our Magnetic North.

Identifying what enables our best self is an important
first step. This includes understanding more about willpower, the power of habits, the keys to resilience, how
we achieve flow, how we capitalize on our strengths, the
power of intrinsic motivation, and what form of charisma
uniquely fits each of us. Closely linked is how we take care

of ourselves. Sleep, movement, and eating well all factor into our stamina, our patience, and our ability to persevere when times get tough. We must take our full self into consideration to be at our best physically, emotionally, and cognitively. It takes courage to live our character each day. Our Magnetic North—the principles by which we live—guide our behavior, allowing us to prioritize when principles inevitably collide.[59]

Identification is based on two components, each equally important. First, we need to identify our internal compass.

The key values that define us at our core determine our path; will we follow our internal compass or follow the compass of others?

Researchers Postmes and Jetten define identity as follows: "Personal identity is defined as 'a person's unique sense of self': the gestalt of idiosyncratic attributes such as traits, abilities, and interests." Identity defines our essence as individuals and the behaviors that arise from that definition.[60]

Firstly, our core values need to be identified. What is most important to us? Bob Quinn, a researcher at the University of Michigan and founder of Positive Organizational Scholarship, calls this being internally directed. He asks the following questions: "What would my story be if I were living up to the values of others? What would I do if I had 10% more integrity than I have right now? How can I live my core values in this situation? What could I do right now to be more authentic? If I were not worried about the negative consequences, what would be the right thing to do?"[61]

Secondly, it is critical for us to identify our destination: what success looks like. The definition of the challenge we face and our hoped-for solution may shift as time goes on, but it must be clearly identified.

Education and confidence give us the keys to our future, set upon a foundation of values. Education and confidence allow us to act as we should—true to our own values and beliefs—and give us charisma inspired by moral courage that cascades to others. This defines our character.

Raising people up is the key to accelerating success. The

greatest satisfaction comes from seeing others succeed, grow, and gain confidence from success. We need to build others up, allowing them to be at their best.[62]

The influence each of us has on those around us is not always apparent, but our actions are. A note I received once said, "You challenged us to be better and we wanted to meet the challenge. We have learned principles not from a book, but from your consistent example. It is easy to respect you."

> The greatest satisfaction comes from seeing others succeed, grow, and gain confidence from success.

What meaningful words! Being a consistent example requires being true to oneself—being internally directed.[63] It shows in all that we do. And, in the end, it leads to connection and respect, a wonderful combination for enhancing the odds of optimizing performance and gaining fulfillment from what we do. Time tests us. We want our Magnetic North to withstand the test of time.

Writing down goals we hope to achieve increases the chance of success tenfold, according to psychologist John Norcross.[64] This is why New Year's resolutions, and all other resolutions, should be written down. Setting goals, regardless of size, improves performance.[65]

Having an entire group adopt a unifying goal is hard but possible. Meaningful goals energize us each day. They make us feel alive. We are working for a good greater than ourselves, and we need to recall that "we have goals—goals don't have us."[66]

Our destination is fueled by successfully defining what we are looking to achieve. Clearly defining a goal is critical to success.[67] As noted earlier, the more complex the challenge, the more detailed the action plan needs to be. We need to define the problem and what we hope the outcome to be.

The goals we are looking to achieve need to be supported with a clear vision, a clear message, and with clear communication in mind. Clarity cannot be emphasized enough. Definition of the challenge—what it is, who it affects, why it is an issue, how much it might cost, where it is, and the like—are all part of clearly defining the scope of the challenge and laying the groundwork for solving it.[68]

Wayne Baker, a researcher at the University of Michigan and author of the foreword to this book and *All You Have to Do Is Ask*, notes: "Having meaningful goals isn't just useful when it comes to identifying needs, it's actually a prescription for satisfaction and happiness in life. Goals provide structure and meaning, purpose and control. Making progress toward meaningful goals gives you confidence. And, pursuing goals often requires you to engage other people and develop positive relationships—which produce happiness." But he goes on to say that not all goals are created equal. "The ones most likely to bring you happiness are intrinsic, meaning you find them inherently interesting, inspiring, and energizing, rather than simply a means to an end."[69]

Identifying the challenge requires self-reflection. Is the challenge in front of us being solved for our own good, for the group's good, or both? Is it to advance our own interests? If it is personal rather than group-based, it will be harder to achieve and harder to create co-owners in the solution. If it is driven by what is good both for oneself and for a group or society, gathering a coalition and achieving success with others is far easier. It is far better to have personal rewards derived from the collective good, rather than putting one's own objectives first. I have seen this first-hand in the employee-owned business (ESOP) community. Having "all oars in the water" pulling in the same direction has an enormous impact on results.

Our goals must include the "why" behind each of them, as the "why" adds depth of understanding and enhances commitment. We need to establish metrics, set milestone dates for completion, and determine the resources needed to achieve our goal—be it information, advice, endorsements, communication, participation, or a referral in addition to financial, physical, and human resources. This is how we begin picturing the future state we seek.[70]

> It can be hard to give up the pride of ownership, but shared ownership leads toward greater opportunities for success.

Doing the right thing for others results in what is right for us as well. In essence, fairness and recognition follow success. Others need to be trusted to put the group first, rather than solely focusing on personal needs. It can be hard to give up the pride of ownership, but shared ownership leads toward greater opportunities for success.

WILLPOWER

» Willpower can be viewed as a MUSCLE. Exercise and planning for inflection points strengthen willpower.

Daniel Lerner and Alan Schlechter. 2017. New York. UThrive. Little, Brown and Company

As we look inward, it helps to understand what can throw us off track: our willpower or motivation weakening, falling back into unproductive habits, or losing our resilient mindset. In order to live our values and be true to our character, we need the strength of perseverance. We need the resolve to continue in spite of headwinds. We need to access our strengths and use them in our daily lives.

Willpower is strongest early in the morning but drains as daily stress mounts. Our willpower is weakest in the evening, which is why it is so easy to grab that salty snack, ice cream, or other favorite food or drink after dinner. Knowing willpower weakens as the day wears on allows us to consider alternate routines. What cognitive reminders can we give ourselves to surpass this willpower deficit?

I know it is much easier for me to avoid salty snacks throughout the day, but my willpower often gives in at the end of the day. Cognitive reminders help me move from an automatic action to a considered action as I reach willpower deficits.

Knowing willpower weakens as the day wears on allows us to consider alternate routines.

Daniel Lerner, a professor at NYU, and Alan Schlechter, MD, authors of *UThrive*, think of willpower as a muscle that can be strengthened. Blood sugar levels, decision-making, multitasking, and lack of sleep all contribute to loss of willpower.[71]

In a study by Florida State University researchers, one group of students were asked to eat radishes, even though cookies were also present. A second group was asked to do the opposite. The cookie eaters had more willpower to problem solve than the radish eaters. By resisting cookies, radish eaters diminished their reserves of willpower.[72]

In another study, researchers had participants watch a video. Candy was placed near some and far from others. Some were told they could eat the candy while others were told they could not. The researchers wanted to determine the effect of willpower on future behavior. As they suspected, those who used more willpower during the video ate more ice cream after the video than those who did not deplete their willpower.[73]

We can strengthen willpower by planning for inflection points, knowing how we plan to respond in those situations.

Scottish psychologists Sheina Orbell and Paschal Sheeran studied patients who were recovering from knee and hip replacement surgeries in 1992—a time when recovery from these surgeries was painful and difficult. The participants in the study were generally in their upper sixties and were similar in background. Each patient was given a booklet with instructions for their rehabilitation; following these instructions was critical to avoid blood clots and scar tissue that could impede movement once the joint fully healed. Half of the patients were asked to write goals for each week during the recovery period in the thirteen blank pages inserted behind the guidelines. Amazingly, those who wrote goals were able to get themselves up from a chair unassisted three weeks faster than the control group, were able to walk two weeks sooner, and could return to normal life activity more quickly.

As Orbell and Sheeran studied those thirteen pages in the back of the recovery plan, they noticed a pattern. Specific plans had been written to deal with inflection points—how to deal with moments of challenge and how the patient would get through those moments. Detailing these plans allowed them to increase their willpower.[74]

A similar study was done by Mark Muraven at the University of Albany. He used warm cookies with college students. Half of the students were given stern commands not to eat the cookies while the other students were treated kindly. The kindly treated students were guided with polite instructions to not eat the cookies and were asked to provide input on any factors they saw that could improve the experiment in the future.

Neither group ate the cookies during the five-minute experiment, however, the willpower needed to perform the following twelve-minute tedious task was dramatically more evident for the students who were treated kindly. As it turns out, the researchers found willpower is enhanced when we believe we have a sense of autonomy or choice. On the other hand, the researchers found the students who were treated abruptly felt drained by the short experience, decreasing their willpower.[75]

The implications of increasing or depleting willpower are substantial. We can strengthen the willpower of others by being kind, considerate, and giving them autonomy. Being near others with good habits also raises our own willpower. As one who had good study habits in college, I noticed new roommates' grades go up when we roomed together. This is "the principle of social proof. It states that one means to determine what is correct is to find out what other people think is correct. The principle applies especially to the way we decide what constitutes correct behavior."[76]

We need to find ways to strengthen our willpower and the willpower of those around us. It helps us be our best selves and stay true to our identity.

Charles Duhigg, in his book *The Power of Habits,* describes what he calls the "habit loop." The habit loop is essentially this: a cue triggers a routine, which in turn, creates a reward. Habits are formed slowly over time. We may not even notice a habit being formed. Habits reduce the energy our brains need to process information. Our reactions become routine, needing little thought.

Habits are incredibly hard to change. Keystone habits, those that are foundational and domino to other aspects of our lives, are the most influential in making a difference (for example, smoking and drinking). So, how do we change habits? Most often, the cue remains constant. However, we can consciously insert a new routine when a cue is received, which can lead to the reward we are seeking. In the case of the Scottish study on knee and hip rehabilitation, participants created strategies to deal with pain points—routines they followed that allowed them to reach their goal.

> Belief is a central tenet in changing habits.

Habits become most embedded when we begin experiencing the reward by anticipating the outcome. If the reward center of the brain generating dopamine, endorphins, serotonin, and oxytocin is triggered, the habit becomes ingrained.

The belief in something that expands beyond oneself is central to changing habits, because it gets us through relapses that often happen when we are subject to stress. Belief is a central tenet in changing habits. If we can positively alter habits by understanding the dynamics of willpower in changing habits, we have a much better chance of altering our actions and driving substantially improved performance.[77]

RESILIENCE

» Personal: Not Me (driven by the situation) v. Me
» Pervasive: Not Everything (limited)
  v. Everything (all aspects of life)
» Permanent: Not Always (temporary)
  v. Always (permanent)

Karen Reivich and Andrew Shatte. 2002. New York. The Resilience Factor. Three Rivers Press.

Resilience is complex. It taps deeply into the science of psychology. How does J. K. Rowling bounce back from depression to write the Harry Potter series? How does Maya Angelou rebound from horrible childhood experiences to become an incredibly successful writer, poet, and civil rights leader? Time and again, people bounce back. How do they do it?[78]

Marty Seligman, a University of Pennsylvania researcher and pioneer of the positive psychology movement, notes we need to 1) not make issues personal, 2) not think of the circumstances as permanent, and 3) not consider issues as all-encompassing and pervasive in all aspects of life. We need to learn to overcome the past.

We need to depersonalize issues and ensure they do not overtake our lives. Specific circumstances cause problems, and the issue is not necessarily always about us. Seligman emphasizes positive emotion, engagement, relationships, meaning, and accomplishment as the cornerstones of positive psychology.[79]

We need to believe we have "control over life . . . can learn from failure . . . that we matter as human beings . . . and that we have real strengths on which we can rely and share."[80] The way we think is key to resilience. Accurate thinking is essential.[81]

Reframing thoughts is a major part of being resilient. Getting out of thinking traps is critical. We should not jump to conclusions or catastrophize—blowing up an issue into the worst possible outcome. An alternative explanation for the circumstance needs to be sought. We need to avoid overstatements like "always" and "never." Oftentimes, we assume the worst. Extreme, all-or-nothing thinking (when the only options are perfection or failure) is not helpful. We need to ask questions that create clarity rather than assuming we caused the issue. Getting out of these thinking traps starts by identifying and labeling the trap.[82]

As a self-confessed worrier when our children were out with the car late at night—even though I trusted them completely—I personally fell into the catastrophe trap many, many times. Knowing this thinking trap exists has helped me be better—not great, but better.

If we are overly harsh on ourselves, we need to consciously minimize that blame and stop continual thoughts in line with "I regret . . ." We can write down what is troubling us and actively write down reasons that prove it is false.[83]

We actually overestimate the time it takes to recover

from setbacks. Scholars call it "affective forecasting." When we experience a setback and estimate the time it will take to recover, researchers have consistently found the actual time to recover as less than the original forecast.[84] The resilience and adaptation of some people gives them the ability to excel even when the odds are against them. It starts with believing in oneself. Mindset matters.[85]

It makes a remarkable difference how we frame our thoughts—even if our progress is not going according to plan. We must interpret events, identify our actions and feelings, put things in perspective, and notice how our mood changes. Then, we can begin reshaping our future actions and reactions to similar circumstances.[86]

> It makes a remarkable difference how we frame our thoughts—even if our progress is not going according to plan.

Olivia Fox Cobane, author of *The Charisma Myth*, was in South America for a presentation. The night before, she could not sleep. The more she tried to sleep, the less she could. Then, she shifted her mindset. What if lack of sleep was exactly what was needed to deliver her most highly engaging talk? The next day, her talk went extremely well. Her mindset changed forever to embrace the moments we are given and not view the outcome to be negatively predestined; results can be incredibly positive when we open our mind to that possibility.[87]

In 1961, one of the all-time baseball greats, Willie Mays, hit four home runs in a game—his greatest game. What most people do not know is that he almost did not play that day, having gotten ill from a midnight order of barbecued ribs the night before. In Mays' words, "I think it's a lesson for kids. You don't have to be 100 percent to have a big day. You can still accomplish a lot."[88] Framing thoughts in a positive way regardless of his circumstance was a key foundation of Willie's spectacular baseball career.

Surprisingly, more than 50 percent of people who go through significant adversity come out the other side stronger and create larger impact. By contrast, 15 percent of people going through significant adversity develop post-traumatic stress disorder, or PTSD. Sheryl Sandberg, author of *Option B* and widowed at a very young age, says post-traumatic growth can come in the form of "finding personal strength, gaining appreciation, forming deeper relationships, discovering more meaning in life, and seeing new possibilities."[89]

> Knowing progress is not strictly linear, that inevitable ups and downs exist, prepares us to persevere with optimism.

Growth comes from transcendence—focusing on the well-being of others in addition to ourselves, being open to ideas, and having hope and optimism. We begin to focus on priorities, eliminating a victim mentality, raising the reliance on ourselves, and deepening our sense of meaning.[90]

Knowing progress is not strictly linear, that inevitable ups and downs exist, prepares us to persevere with optimism. Staying calm rubs off on others. Someone once said to me, "Things are calmer whenever you arrive." The influence we have on others matters. Resilient thinking can aid those around us.

Being resilient improves both physical and mental health. It changes the way we think, transforming challenges into problems to be solved, hardships into learning experience. It takes energy, discipline, and commitment. We must focus on our strengths and believe that change is possible.[91]

In Angela Duckworth's *Grit*, she notes people gravitate toward innate ability as the explanation for exceptional performance (think Michael Jordan). This limits our need to compare ourselves to those achieving extraordinary results— we can consider it exceptional talent, rather than a result of the resilience it takes to get it done.

Duckworth points out that skill is the product of talent and effort. Achievement is the product of skill and effort. Effort is the common denominator. Without talent and effort, achievement is not possible.[92] To this, Positive Organizational Scholarship gives us the research basis for exceptional performance—allowing skill, ability, and effort to complement the foundational elements that are critical in our efforts to optimize performance.

> We should do what we love, not what others love.

Robert Vallerand of Northwestern University extends the concept of grit through passion, noting passion can be either harmonious or obsessive. Psychological well-being, physical well-being, relationships, contribution to society, and performance all peak with harmonious passion through positive emotions, persistence, and mindfulness. If passion becomes obsessive, it can lead to faltering relationships, reduced physical wellbeing, and poorer performance. Harmonious passion generates energy. Obsessive passion can cause a loss of energy. We should do what we love, not what others love.[93]

Every change, personal or professional, requires resilience. If we practice accurately interpreting adversity, recognize our emotions, know the importance of effort, and put the circumstance in perspective, we can change our energy, elevating our progress and that of those around us.

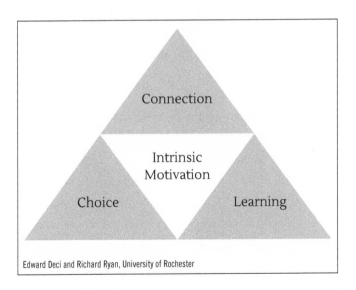

Edward Deci and Richard Ryan, University of Rochester

Intrinsic motivation is at the center of high performance. What drives us? Why do we do what we do? How can we move from within rather than act out of compliance? When we are intrinsically motivated, we enjoy the journey and find it inherently more satisfying. The activity is reward in and of itself. Unlike extrinsic motivation, intrinsic motivation does not simply focus on the finish line—be it fame, wealth, beauty, power, praise, or other extrinsic rewards. Extrinsic motivation focuses on outward measures of success. When we are intrinsically motivated, we take ownership of what we are doing. We become able to enjoy the journey, not just the destination.[94]

Edward Deci and Richard Ryan at the University of Rochester have determined intrinsic motivation to be based on the pillars of learning/competence/growth, autonomy/independence/choice, and personal connection/belonging. Motivation suffers when growth, independence, and belonging are not present.[95]

I always thought that I was born with a double dose of intrinsic motivation: I was driven and focused, and for years and years, I was highly motivated. Then, one day, it was gone. It vanished. Activities that used to be easy became hard. I was drained. I had to make changes so my intrinsic motivation bounced back. Studying Deci and Ryan's work made me realize: learning was the spark that ignited me.

Soon after these crucial changes to my mentality, my energy returned. My enthusiasm and stamina returned. I was having fun again, and I was learning more than I had in decades. It created the path that led me to study

Positive Organizational Scholarship and, ultimately, write this book.

Deci states that a feeling of competence—gaining mastery—is essential in fueling intrinsic motivation.[96] We all gravitate toward the things we do well. I remember being given self-study textbooks on mathematics in the eighth grade; I charged through three full textbooks over the course of the year, gaining great satisfaction from the journey and knowing I was the master over my own learning speed. We all have areas in which we excel, getting into the flow of the moment.

Bradley Staats, a researcher at the University of North Carolina and author of *Never Stop Learning*, has done extensive work on how we learn. He breaks down learning into the two forms originally conceived by Chris Argyris, a former emeritus professor at the Harvard Business School. Single-loop learning is what we experience every day as we solve problems. Double-loop learning requires reflection, and it is where the most significant gains are made. In double-loop learning we look at cause and effect; we look at the process and make system-based improvements.

> Being too busy to reflect reduces the power of learning.

Reflection is the key to maximizing our learning. The simple act of reflecting and writing down two lessons learned can improve performance by 10 percent or more. Being too busy to reflect reduces the power of learning.[97]

People want choice. No one wants to be told what to

do. When we become actively involved in the choices we make, we become intrinsically motivated.[98]

In Angela Duckworth's *Grit*, she describes experiments done in the 1960s on influencing destiny. These experiments were done initially with dogs (when it was legal to do so) and later repeated with rats. In each case, pain was created via shock. One group could end the shock by learning a specific behavior. The other group had no choice.

> Autonomy, the willingness to act of our own free will, increases effectiveness and allows for more creative solutions.

In each case, those that had no control became submissive. When the shock occurred, they endured—most giving no effort to influence the outcome. However, in the groups that knew behavior could change the outcome, they sought a solution for ending the pain—and did so successfully.[99]

David Cooperrider, a researcher at Case Western University and pioneer of appreciative inquiry, has said, "People don't resist change. They resist being changed."[100] The locus of control is different. If it comes from within, we are motivated by it, we take initiative and control. If it comes from the outside, we push against compliance. Allowing others to participate in the process elevates intrinsic motivation; it starts with allowing choice, which simultaneously strengthens trust. Self-motivated behavior sustains itself. Autonomy, the willingness to act of our own free will, increases effectiveness and allows for more creative solutions.

The concept of autonomy facilitates goal-setting, monitoring progress, and achieving those goals. Every one of us wants to author our own actions. When we align our actions with our core values, we become fully absorbed in an activity and feel that our personal actions are leading to a positive result.

Autonomy does not mean an absence of guardrails. If challenges are too great, anxiety and ineffectiveness result. If challenges are too easy, boredom sets in. Striking the right balance of capability and challenge maximizes intrinsic motivation.[101]

Personal connection is the third pillar of intrinsic motivation. High quality connections increase innovative thinking, openness, curiosity, and the love of learning. We are not intrinsically motivated solely by our own self-interests. Rather, intrinsic motivation is heightened when we contribute to the well-being of others.[102]

The concept of intrinsic motivation also applies to children. Research shows five key ingredients in creating self-motivated behavior. Parents need to let children know what is expected of them; children need to know their parents are fully present; they need to know they participate with an element of choice (even though consequences may follow if they exercise choice in a way that is not productive); children must feel the parent trusts them; and lastly, they need a challenge that matches their skill level, including elevation as their skill level increases.[103]

What applies to children applies equally to adults. These five concepts are the formula for intrinsic motivation.

We must have choice. We must trust our environment and our ability to resolve a challenge. We need the challenge to be well defined and to know others are fully present with us.

Considering the perspective of others feeds intrinsic motivation. Simply put, activating intrinsic motivation in others is an overriding key to making an impact. Doing as we are told (being compliant) or being pressured to act in a certain way (being controlled) conflicts with intrinsic motivation and can lead to defiance.[104]

Intrinsic motivation is maximized when creating an environment that emphasizes choice, flexibility, freedom, autonomy, learning, and a connection with others that supports alignment of our innermost values. It requires looking at issues as challenges to be solved rather than problems that cause headaches. It requires support and praise for others doing their best, rather than being judgmental and evaluative. Truly tapping into our intrinsic motivation—generating satisfaction that comes from self-improvement—and understanding the intrinsic motivation of others creates an environment where hierarchy becomes secondary and progress feels both natural and self-determined:[105]

> Simply put, activating intrinsic motivation in others is an overriding key to making an impact.

> Surgeons say that during a difficult operation they have a sensation that the entire operating team is a single organism, moved by the same purpose; they describe it

as "ballet" in which the individual is subordinated to the performance of the group, and all involved share a feeling of harmony and power.[106]

It is this concept of Teamflow that is so powerful. When we create the ability to understand challenges through the perspective of others, we create order that enlivens and motivates us.

What we strive for is harmonic convergence creating unity based on active listening, adapting and, ultimately, achieving a state of flow. We do, however, need to be aware of the challenges of having both intrinsic and extrinsic goals.

Having multiple motives actually decreases our ability to achieve our goals. A study by Yale School of Management researcher Amy Wrzesniewski of ten thousand West Point cadets showed that those motivated intrinsically had more career success than those who were motivated by a combination of intrinsic (internal drive) and extrinsic (i.e., recognition, praise) factors.

> Having multiple motives actually decreases our ability to achieve our goals.

In another research study with small children, "yummy" crackers were more motivating than those that were described as "yummy" and that also "make you strong." Performance can be undermined by having both intrinsic and extrinsic factors driving our desire to succeed.[107]

We all have times in our lives when we are firing on all cylinders and lose ourselves in the moment. Time disappears. Minutes seem like hours and hours seem like minutes. Our concentration levels are high, shielding us from noise and distractions. We feel as though we have control or the possibility of control. Our goal is larger than our personal interest alone, we have clear, unambiguous rules, and our discipline feels effortless. We are open to learning, and the challenge at hand is neither too easy nor too difficult based on our skill. And, we enjoy the journey toward the destination. When this happens, we have achieved a state of "flow" as researched and defined by Mihaly Csíkszentmihályi, a distinguished professor of psychology and management at Claremont Graduate University and author of *Flow*.

> In this state, what we do is effortless; it allows us to achieve the unexpected.

In order to achieve flow, we need to know a task has a chance of being completed, have a clear goal, get immediate feedback, and have a sense of control. In this state, what we do is effortless; it allows us to achieve the unexpected. We build self-confidence and concern for others, are highly disciplined and spontaneous, and we find meaningful, harmonic patterns to motivate us to learn and keep on learning.[108]

Some of us experience periods of flow virtually every day; time warps around those moments. But flow does not just cover those few instances in life when everything clicks and you achieve extraordinary results. Those moments are tremendous, but so are the everyday flow moments that make our days enjoyable and fuel our motivation.

Personally, I love moments of flow. These moments create the best experiences through every aspect of my life—be it at work, at home, playing sports, or simply laughing with friends and family.

To unlock our potential, researcher Amy Wrzesniewski created the concept of job crafting. We each have strengths, and job crafting points us to including those strengths in all that we do. If we look at every role we play, we can alter how they are done to maximize our satisfaction and effectiveness. Job crafting can make our work more meaningful and interesting. It can connect our work to our personal meaning and purpose. Job crafting increases engagement, job satisfaction, and resilience. It allows us to fit our personal values into our work.[109]

> When we measure ourselves, we should measure ourselves against our inherent potential, not based on limitations or the perception of others.

A study of almost ten thousand people conducted by Lucy Hone, the director of the New Zealand Institute of Well-being and Resilience at the University of Canterbury, demonstrated we are nine times more likely to be flourishing when we know our strengths than when we don't. When we utilize our strengths, we are eighteen times more likely to flourish than those that are not actively using their strengths.[110] This is another big take-away: know and use your strengths.

I enjoy writing, photography, and attempting to make complex issues easy to understand. When I am doing my work, if I can incorporate these elements, my satisfaction rises considerably. We each have interests and strengths. Our work will be better and more satisfying if we can build them into our daily lives to even the smallest extent.

When we measure ourselves, we should measure ourselves against our inherent potential, not based on limitations or the perception of others. We all need to view possibilities of what can be, not what isn't yet. We need to view life through the lens of abundance.[111]

Our strengths are not always obvious to others. For example, take this profile description for a player in the National Football League: "Poor build, skinny, lacks great physical stature and strength, lacks mobility and ability to avoid the rush, lacks a really strong arm, can't drive the ball downfield, does not throw a really tight spiral . . . can get exposed if forced to ad lib."[112] Why would any NFL team draft a player with this profile? The list of unlikely NFL draft characteristics does not stop with this description. Underachieving running backs, linebackers, receivers, and cornerbacks all follow the same theme. Chris Hogan, a former lacrosse player turned wide receiver, explained to the *New York Times*: "The idea is to make you better at what you already do well."

This is exactly what strength-based Teamflow is all about. It is just one aspect of the success of the New England Patriots over the course of nearly twenty years. Focusing on putting people in a position to utilize those strengths, rather than improving weaknesses, is a core tenet of Positive Organizational Scholarship.

Tom Brady, a future Hall of Fame quarterback, shared his dismal scouting report a number of years ago. However, he was assembled into a strength-based system. Antwan Smith, Matt Light, David Patton, David Givens, Corey Dillon, Malcolm Butler, Matt Chatham, and Matt Hogan all utilized their strengths to help the team succeed. In an environment that seeks parity, the NFL, seeing the Patriots focus on roles that give players the best chance of success underscores why they have been so good for so long.[113]

Using their example, can we identify our strengths and reshape our roles to maximize the strengths on our team? My sister-in-law is a retired elementary school teacher. She would have her students decorate puzzle pieces with words, pictures, and symbols that represent their personal attributes. Then, the puzzle pieces are put together on a bulletin board in her classroom. It shows the children that each of them has strengths; the students come together as a team, each contributing a different, but important, piece of the puzzle.

> The sum of our strength is so much greater than any individual strength we have.

The sum of our strength is so much greater than any individual strength we have. Power exists in capturing the collective strengths of all members of a group.

Charisma captures the essence of how we connect with and impact others. It is critical in all that we do. We sometimes think charisma is hereditary, but the reality is we have the strength to form and utilize our own kind of charisma. We need to recognize it in ourselves and harness its benefits.

Presence charisma is characterized by listening skill, mental focus, and attentive body language. Power and authority charisma comes from expertise, intelligence, confidence, or status. Visionary charisma makes us believe in something larger than ourselves.[114] Michele Obama notes in her book *Becoming*, "There is something innately bolstering about a person that sees opportunities as endless."[115] Kindness charisma holds power through goodwill, gratitude, and compassion. Some of us can flex between charisma styles. For others, one form is primary.

Each form of charisma is powerful. We must be aware of the types of charisma that can accentuate the effect we have on others. Some, like kindness charisma, should be used when delivering bad news, because it creates an emotional connection. People feel valued and important. When conveying hope, tapping into visionary charisma is important.[116]

Whether we realize it or not, we are constantly "selling" our thoughts and ideas. Charisma helps us do this. Daniel Pink, in *To Sell Is Human*, speaks to authenticity. When others see the passion we have for a goal, when we present it with empathy, and when we are honest and transparent, it can take hold. He quotes, "Do we have the capability to step outside [our] own experience and imagine the emotions, perceptions, and motivations of another?"[117]

Our ability to personally thrive is created through a combination of learning and vitality, as shown by University of Michigan researcher, Gretchen Spreitzer. This is the state of positive energy we all seek. It is the moment when "flow" happens—being so immersed that the passage of time seems to disappear. It is our highest state. We are engaged physically (nutrition, sleep, and fitness), emotionally (inspired and motivated) and mentally (focused and attentive). It is the condition when we are feeling alive and focused on learning and innovation. We are co-creating contagious energy that rejuvenates us, cascading positive spirals of thought and action in an environment of civility and high relational energy. Challenge, respect, autonomy, and the opportunity to learn all connect to ignite and enable us.[118]

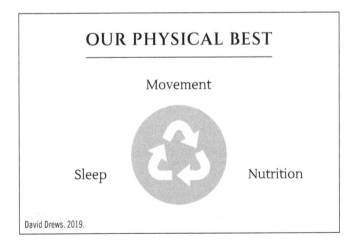

OUR PHYSICAL BEST

Movement

Sleep

Nutrition

David Drews. 2019.

As we reflect on what creates our best self, we need to consider the physical aspects of life that give us strength. If we are not at our best, how can we catalyze others to be their best? And how will we have the stamina and patience to face and resolve challenges to our value system? We need to restore ourselves.

For example, so many of us do not get enough sleep. Forty percent of Americans get less than seven hours of sleep a night. According to the National Sleep Foundation, nearly 30 percent of Americans got less than six hours of sleep on the previous day.[119] And only a small percentage genetically need little sleep.[120] I know I am one of the vast majority that needs sleep.

Spreitzer's research on sleep shows that the lack thereof reduces focus, increases stress, and lowers the quality of work. Sleep allows our minds to process and sort information for decision-making, codes information into our long-term memory, and improves our ability to concentrate.[121]

> Sleep makes us better cognitively, emotionally, and physically.

Sleep is good for our brains. Sleep makes us better cognitively, emotionally, and physically. We make wiser decisions. Former president Bill Clinton once said that every significant mistake he made was tied to lack of sleep. Sleep lowers anxiety, depression, and shortness of temper while improving our memory capacity, competence, concentration, situational awareness, reaction time, attention span, and memory.[122]

Naps as short as six minutes increase our memory

performance; naps also boost our immune system, increase our learning power, and raise cognitive performance. Daniel Pink points out in his book *When* that the ideal nap is between ten and twenty minutes in length, preceded by caffeine, since caffeine takes about twenty-five minutes to enter the bloodstream. These short naps have immediate benefit without the initial groggy feeling that can come from longer naps. Sleep lowers our risk of being sedentary, smoking, and maintaining a poor diet. It also improves our mood and our wellbeing.[123]

Behavioral factors like activity level, caffeine, weight, and alcohol use all impact our ability to sleep. Environmental factors like daylight, blue light from electronic devices, noise, and electronic media are easier to control than work schedules. Factors like worry and stress reduce our ability to sleep.[124] Kindness and gratitude at the end of our day are calming and facilitate a good night's sleep. This can be facilitated by a gratitude journal, described in chapter 4.[125]

The brain comprises 2 percent of body weight but consumes 20 percent of the body's energy intake. We have heard it many times before: eat more fruits, vegetables, beans, fish, grains, and nuts. Dietary guidance calls for 50 percent vegetables, 25 percent healthy starch, and 25 percent protein.[126] Nutrition is the fuel that helps propel us to be our best.

Five places on Earth have ten times the number of people who reach age one hundred than in the United States. These places vary widely in location—from Nicoya,

Costa Rica to Ikaria, Greece; Sardinia, Italy to Okinawa, Japan. In each of these locations, the diet relies on heavily plant-based food.

In Okinawa, Japan, the people have long eaten in moderation, following the ancient tradition of eating until they are 80 percent full. The precise reason why this practice seems to slow aging is not yet known.[127]

Even if we do not follow the 80-percent-full tradition of the people of Okinawa, we can focus on eating in moderation and looking at the quality of our diet. I know that I personally feel physically different after eating a healthy meal versus one filled with deep-fried or otherwise unhealthy food. We can consciously monitor how we feel based on what we eat and improve our energy level by following a diet that is more intuitive.

Movement is good for the mind and body. Being active your way creates sustainable habits. Aerobic exercise, flexibility, resistance, and balance training all sum to the best physical condition. Movement in the face of day-to-day work and family time constraints can be difficult—and is easy to drop off the daily "to do" list. Thankfully, Fitbit and other step-counters are making it easier to measure activity and provide a means of "group think"—using the camaraderie of friends to encourage greater physical activity.

In Michelle Segar's research on movement at the University of Michigan, she has found that when emotion is engaged, the sustainability of our desire to move increases dramatically. If we move to lose weight, lower cholesterol, or some other clinical factor, movement is generally not sustainable. However, if we tie joy to our movement, treating the experience as an energizing experience, an opportunity to grow our creativity, help our focus, or increase our connection to others, the activity can more easily sustain itself. We are better off engaging emotion. Emotion is more powerful than the rational part of our brain. We need to engage emotion in order to increase the probability movement becomes a part of our everyday lives.

> Emotion is more powerful than the rational part of our brain.

Segar notes that movement is cumulative. All movement is good. It is additive. We should look for "Opportunities to Move." We can incorporate walking into our days and get steps in while we are on phone calls. Movement helps generate energy—especially if quick exposure to the outdoors is possible.

Negativity—being "off" on a given day—is so much more powerful than positivity. If we are at our best, others can feed off the energy and optimize their own performance without being impeded by negativity.[128]

In the end, eating well, sleeping well, and movement help each of us to be at our best. Teamflow requires us to be at our best physically if we are going to enable others to be at their best.

When I was in my thirties, I worked extremely hard. On one particular evening, after having been out for a long dinner, I came home and went directly to bed. An hour later, my heart raced out of control. I woke my wife because I thought I was having a heart attack. I panicked. She called 911 and our neighbor came, provided support, and watched our children as I was loaded into the ambulance. After a series of tests, it was determined to be a panic attack.

I never wanted to experience that feeling again. The doctor first said I could choose one of two ways to reverse or stop future attacks. On a cold winter night, I could open the window and draw long breaths from the frigid cold air—that should stop it. He also said if I exercised regularly, I never would have another episode.

This alarm was one of the greatest gifts God could have ever given me. I had always watched my diet but had not made time for exercise. More than twenty-five years later, I still regularly exercise. It builds stamina for both the body and the mind. It gives us time to think and allows us to be at our best, enabling us to cast positive ions to others and help them be their best. The doctor was right. Thankfully, I never had another panic attack.

Segar, who also researches science-based systems for sustainable health behavior change, tells in her book the story of an exercise client's perspective changing. This client intentionally chose a "drill sergeant" instructor as a personal trainer. Near the end of the workout, a run was required up a steep hill. The client dreaded it and complained to Segar about having to do it.

Segar urged her client to take control—walk, run, or don't do it. It was his choice. When Segar saw the client again, a smile brimmed. The client had chosen to run up that hill. It was his choice—a motivating choice. It was no longer a burden but a personal choice.[129]

We need to take control of our nutrition, movement, and sleep patterns. By allowing ourselves to elevate our physical wellbeing, we give ourselves the best chance of raising our performance and the performance of those around us.

In the end, we need courage to be our best selves. Courage is not the absence of fear, but rather the ability to act in the face of fear. At times, people are so intent on proving they are right that they forget what is right. These situations test our moral courage and become testimony to the values we hold. Having the courage to be true to our values takes continuous resolve.

> By allowing ourselves to elevate our physical wellbeing, we give ourselves the best chance of raising our performance and the performance of those around us.

Courage isn't always physical. Entrepreneurs face the world with courage every day, believing they can make an impact, as do teachers. We have all seen the courage of countless front line pandemic workers—from health care professionals to first responders to workers in essential industries—who have aided each of us during the COVID-19 pandemic. Countless others show courage every day as well. It takes courage and confidence to guide oneself and others toward thriving and fulfillment.

It is through reflection and resolve that we make our greatest impact: the courage to try something new, to get

back up and try again when we fail, or to face and sub-
due fear. Courage, perseverance, and positive attitude are an
unstoppable combination.

Values are the cornerstone, the starting place. Without
values, we run with the crowd. Here are just some characteristics of identity: ethical, empathetic, encouraging,
other-centric, authentic, courageous, truthful, persistent,
relational, confident, optimistic, adaptable, and fair. These
are anchor values. If they are part of our makeup, we may
fall short on them from time to time, but they will shine
through in the marathon of life.

Out of this group of concepts, I struggled most with
the word "courageous." Many of us do not typically think of
ourselves in that way. We think of Seal Team Six members
and the men and women who took down United Flight 93
over Pennsylvania on September 11, 2001, as courageous.
Based on that definition, we do not fit.

When I made my latest transition in life, one that led to
writing this book, a friend said, "Of all the things you have
done in life, this is the most courageous." He knew how
hard it would be to walk away from the known and into the
unknown. It is a different form of courage; one I had not
previously considered. Recognizing a next phase of life took
reflection, and this kind of deep change is hard. We have to
believe in ourselves, to follow our instincts in order to chart
the course of our future.

Atul Gawande, best-selling author and physician, notes
that focus is the greatest when perception exists that time is

finite. It is true. This realization allowed me to move on and look for a different way to make an impact.[130]

None of us will achieve each and every one of our personal identity qualities every day. They should be aspirational. They should be directional. They should guide us and allow us to learn and adapt when we fall short. They should serve as our Magnetic North, be the rock on which our character stands.

Sometimes, the trust we place in others is broken. Trust is fragile. When principles collide, we need to know our hierarchy for decisions. Selfless behavior draws out the best in others, but selfish behavior drains the energy of those around us.

During the pandemic, I experienced this firsthand. A small group, looking to exercise what they believed to be their individual rights, did not consider the impact those actions would have on a group of peers. Though they said they would never do anything to hurt the peer group, their actions were set to do exactly that. I confronted them on this contradiction with a face-to-face, passionate plea. In this moment, I did not cower. I did not swear. I was driven by and lived my values. I placed the good of the group ahead of individual interests. Though emotion ran very high, ultimately, they made the right choice and backed down.

Standing true to your principles and values in the heat of the moment is hard. It requires doing what is right, not what is easy. When we act in a manner consistent with our character, peace envelopes us. Alignment with our values keeps our personal harmony intact.

Authenticity is the capstone. An authentic person is accepted and endeared. Respect is so much more powerful than hierarchical authority, because it binds us together. Authenticity is a natural extension of trust. Deeply caring about others allows an expression of genuine interest that permeates those around us. Authenticity fosters the ability to work toward the collective good.

Certain people shine through with authentic character that is lived daily. Pope Francis is one of those people, and it is clear for all to see. He embodies empathy and kindness. He does not fall for the trappings of wealth or authority. He connects with people of every race, is rooted in love, and lives his life in accord with his authentic self.

> Authenticity fosters the ability to work toward the collective good.

We will not all achieve this level of authenticity. We can all strive to display our true selves, in good times and in challenging times. It is the fabric that defines us. Behavioral integrity—action, not words—allows others to know what we stand for. When we change behaviors, attitude follows.[131]

Victor Stecher, researcher and author of *Life on Purpose*, encourages us to "stop being afraid and start being yourself."[132] Each of us define who we are from the inside out each and every day.

When I was a senior at Michigan State University, I accepted a job auditing the Game and Fish Fund. This is the fund that holds all fishing and hunting license proceeds. It is earmarked for the sole benefit of hunting and fishing. A watchdog group did not believe the funds were being managed properly, so I was hired to audit the fund.

I quickly realized it was an overwhelming job. There was no way I could properly audit the fund, part time, in six months' time. I asked an auditor who had been in the field for decades for advice. He said to limit the scope, be clear on the objective, and stay focused.

Armed with this knowledge, I stood firm on narrowing the scope with the watchdog group. We identified the highest risk areas. I set out to interview state employees. Remarkably, state employees were as disillusioned as the watchdog group. Through the audit, they felt they could expose what was wrong in the organization without exposing themselves to job loss.

Before graduation, the Drews Report was the cover story of a magazine published by the Michigan United Conservation Club. It likely contributed to the resignation of the Director of the Department of Natural Resources.

For me, it simply righted a wrong, as the state was shying away from transparency. As an avid fisherman, I wanted to help make it right. Defining and clarifying what I was looking to achieve was critical in making an impact.

Whistleblowers are the epitome of putting their values first.

When Tyler Shultz, the grandson of former United

States Secretary of State George Shultz, went to work for Theranos, a blood testing company with the goal of revolutionizing the industry, he would never have thought the company was falsifying test results. The company claimed more than two hundred and forty diseases could be identified with a pinprick of blood, rather than through traditional methods.

Tyler never would have thought the former Secretary of State would ignore his pleas for intervention, or that the founder, Elizabeth Holmes, would ignore his concerns. In fact, the founder only took a meeting with him because his grandfather was on the Board of Directors.

Tyler Shultz was right. He stood strong, based on his moral values. In a November 2016 *Wall Street Journal* article, he stated: "Fraud is not a trade secret . . . I refuse to allow bullying, intimidation, and threat of legal action to take away my First Amendment right to speak out against wrongdoing."

The cost was high for him and his parents, who were forced to take loans against their home to protect him legally from intense confrontation with the billion-dollar corporation.

In the end, Tyler Shultz took on the fight and won.[133] In January 2022, Elizabeth Holmes was convicted on three counts of fraud and one count of conspiracy.[134]

To do what Tyler Shultz did takes conviction. It takes perseverance. It takes courage. It takes accepting risk—both personal and financial. He should be commended for living his values.

When I joined Arthur Andersen in 1982, it was one of the most prestigious accounting firms in the world. Today, I introduce myself as having worked in a Big 4 firm or, sometimes, "at Arthur Andersen, when they were reputable." What happened? How did they get so far off key that the entire firm collapsed? What errors in judgment did they have? Similarly, it disappoints me that so many universities ignored complaints and did not uncover the horrible abuse caused by coaches and members of their medical teams.

Stars sometimes blind us. Those with prestige can mask bad behavior or push back on allegations to protect themselves. Unfortunately, not all those in the chain of command look deep enough to get to the heart of the issue. Errors result. Sadly, lives are deeply affected. Core values must take control to root out these problems. We must look to our inner values and live them; we must not be blinded by those we know, those who have power, or those who use the gift of charisma for the wrong reasons. We must have the courage to stand true in difficult times. It is not easy. Knowing and living our values is the first step.

Lao Tzu said it best: "Watch your thoughts, they become your words; watch your words, they become your actions; watch your actions, they become your habits; watch your habits, they become your character; watch your character, it becomes your destiny."[135]

Our destiny ultimately manifests itself in our thoughts and words. Consciously knowing our values allows us to follow our compass toward Magnetic North—honoring values in our words and actions that harmoniously sync our innermost thoughts with our destiny.

Each of us need to define ourselves. All we do reflects on our reputation—our own identity. The composite mosaic of our thoughts, words, and behaviors determines our habits, values, and destiny. It is imperative we find our own.

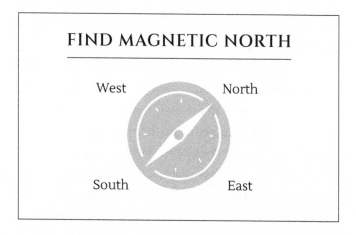

FIND MAGNETIC NORTH

West   North

South   East

Knowing "Magnetic North" on our compass is critically important. When we need to make a critical decision, will we be internally directed or follow the crowd? What will guide our moral compass? Strength comes from resolve. We need to resolve to be our best—honest and true to our innermost core.

Integrity means doing the right thing, even when it is difficult. Living with integrity is hard. It takes character. Protecting one's reputation—and the collective reputation of those around us—is preserved when we are true to our Magnetic North.

As President Woodrow Wilson once said, "If you lose your wealth, you have lost nothing; If you lose your health, you have lost something; but, if you lose your character, you have lost everything."[136]

> The composite mosaic of our thoughts, words, and behaviors determines our habits, values, and destiny.

Chapter 3

IMPACT: MEANING

"Find your truth, an idea which you can live for."
—Søren Kierkegaard, adapted from *Life on Purpose*[137]

Meaning is the source of our passion and inspiration. It is the "why" at the core of our actions. "How" and "what" are secondary. Meaning and purpose give us a sense of providence, destiny, and hope.[138] An anonymous quote said it this way: "The two most important days of your life are the day you are born and the day you find out why."[139]

Bob Quinn, a founder of Positive Organizational Scholarship, has defined his purpose in three words: "Inspire Positive Change." He notes that finding purpose is so much more impactful than going through our lives with an emphasis solely on solving problems. Purpose provides direction for our internal compass. Our lives are created each day. Purpose guides us, it motivates us through a connection to something bigger than ourselves and our personal interests.[140]

Having meaning adds years to our lives. It decreases the risk of heart attack and stroke, reduces the risk of Alzheimer's, diminishes inflammation, increases good cholesterol, doubles the chance of staying drug- or alcohol-free after rehabilitation, relaxes us by day and improves sleep at night, and improves us psychologically and socially. Not having meaning and purpose in our lives increases use of tobacco, contributes toward a poor diet, raises our level of inactivity, and increases stress.[141]

> Our happiness, fulfillment, and energy are best when we live a life filled with purpose.

Victor Strecher, author of *Life on Purpose* and a professor of health behavior and health education at the University of Michigan, notes how purpose acts in the same way as a miracle drug.[142] It exists. We just need to find it in ourselves and others. Our happiness, fulfillment, and energy are best when we live a life filled with purpose.

If we are rooted in helping each other and maintaining a positive mindset guided by meaning and purpose, we will advance collectively and personally. Meaning is the ultimate form of pro-social motivation.

Meaning is powerful. It moves us. It gives us a reason to press on in spite of long odds. It allows us to make a difference and find incredible motivation. Meaning adds depth to life and links the past, present, and future. As Daniel Pink points out in *When*, "The highest function of the future is to enhance the significance of the present."[143] Though we cannot predict the future, we have the ability to create it.

This is another major take-away: Seek to identify your life's purpose. It will lift you up. Try writing it down, brainstorm, rewrite it—let your thoughts flow over and over again. Once it settles into three, four, or five words, continue to refine it. Look back. Look forward. As it gets closer and closer to its final phrase, it will be a constant, persistent thread that will spark motivation for the future.

When I was in public accounting, some joked about green-colored glasses. I did not connect to meaning in my work—we were just auditors. Then, the collapse of Enron and Arthur Andersen awakened the accounting firms. They began taking employees' inspiration regarding the value of their work seriously. They now talk about protecting the financial integrity of the entire financial system and protecting life savings. It is a purpose. Frankly, when I heard how they described it, I felt proud to be an accountant.

KPMG has done a terrific job shifting perspectives from doing audits to protecting life savings. KPMG showed employees how the firm participated in incredible moments of world history, their assistance to the US under FDR to manage the Lend-Lease Act, contributing to the defeat of the Nazis, working in South Africa to verify the election of Nelson Mandela, and monitoring the rebuilding of Ground Zero in New York after September 11. Among many other milestones, KPMG helped prevent fraud during rebuilding after Hurricane Sandy.

KPMG challenged team members to share stories of how each of them impact their clients and their community. They received forty-two thousand responses from twenty-seven thousand employees—an overwhelming result in just a few short months.

Obviously, a latent appetite for purpose in work existed at KPMG. The ability to engage both the mind and heart led to compelling storytelling that was both peer-to-peer and viral by giving employees the opportunity to "like" other employees' stories. Leadership was very involved, helping to create a theme that could be individualized, rather than using scripted mission statements that might be committed to memory, but would not deeply touch each person. Turnover is down. Engagement, discretionary effort, and pride are up.[144]

Survey after survey shows that purpose makes an impact. In a Calling Brands survey, only compensation and benefits ranked higher than purpose.[145] In a Net Impact survey, nearly 50 percent of employees stated they would take a 15 percent pay cut to work for a firm in which their personal purpose connected with the purpose of that firm. Purpose matters.[146]

A few years ago, a student with Asperger's Syndrome fell into deep depression following a candid discussion at school of the effect of climate change on the world—so deep that she barely spoke for months, and her growth was stunted from her lack of appetite. But then she began to research the issue. Slowly, she gained strength. Quietly, she gained resolve.

She took the bold step of deciding to create a climate strike at the grounds of the Swedish capital. She skipped school, saying, "Since adults don't give a damn about my future, I won't either . . . We can't just continue living as if there was no tomorrow, because there is a tomorrow." It is a simple truth delivered by a teenage girl in a fateful moment. Unless we agree on transformative action to reduce greenhouse gas emissions, the world's temperature rise since the Industrial Revolution will hit the 1.5 degrees Celsius mark—an eventuality that scientists warn will expose some 350 million additional people to drought and push nearly 120 million people into extreme poverty by 2030. For every fraction of a degree that temperatures rise, these problems will worsen. This is not fear-mongering, this is science.

After a day of striking alone for climate change, Greta was joined by a stranger. Momentum built into a movement. Millions of people around the world demonstrated. Awareness increased. Climate policies changed in countries around the world. Greta Thurnburg found her life's meaning. "Her moral clarity inspired other young people around the world."[147]

The early years start with an interest, the middle years focus on practicing that interest, and the later years develop purpose and meaning.

Though purpose can be found at an early age, Angela Duckworth points out in *Grit* that purpose is often discovered in our later years. Psychologist Benjamin Bloom noticed the early years start with an interest, the middle years focus on practicing that interest, and the later years develop purpose and meaning.[148]

At the commencement address of Northwestern University in June 2017, Matthew Forti, US Managing Director of One Acre Fund and a recent Northwestern graduate, shared how the fund has helped small-scale African farmers increase yield and make a better living by providing input, financing, training, and better access to markets. One Acre Fund helped more than 450,000 families to end chronic hunger for 1.5 million children—an amazing outcome that has led to health improvements, better education, and community investment. One Acre Fund has been recognized as one of the most innovative companies in Africa by Fast Company and as a top 15 NGO in the *Global Journal.*

Like Greta Thurnburg, Matthew Forti saw the impact he could make at a very young age. He worked in consulting even while helping found the One Acre Fund. He moved to One Acre Fund full time when its order of magnitude needed a full-time director. Such clarity at a young age is not always evident.[149]

Sometimes, life only makes sense when we look back through time and connect the dots. Viewed thus, our purpose can be woven through all we do.

At the commencement address of our son at the University of Michigan, we heard Larry Brilliant, MD, speak. His story was truly amazing and inspiring.

When Dr. Brilliant was at the University of Michigan

for his undergraduate work, his father was fighting cancer. As a result, Brilliant was feeling low. He happened to attend a small gathering in Hill Auditorium where a young progress maker, Dr. Martin Luther King Jr., was making a case for equal civil rights. Dr. Brilliant met Dr. King. He marched with Dr. King on multiple occasions, and he spent time in jail as a result of his marching and support for civil rights.

Helping the less fortunate took Dr. Brilliant to Alcatraz in the 1960s. When a call went out to help a pregnant Native American woman, he answered the call. He stayed and became the doctor for a group of Native Americans called All Tribes. He spoke with the press. He gained notoriety.

After Alcatraz, he was invited to play a small role in a motion picture filming in Los Angeles. He was paid in the form of an airline ticket, and off he went to Europe. When a cyclone hit Bangladesh, he followed his instinct and went to help. When civil unrest stopped the relief efforts, he went to a Himalayan ashram, Neem Karoli Baba, in India. Here he met Steve Jobs.

Neem Karoli Baba told Dr. Brilliant that he needed to make a difference in the world by eradicating smallpox, one of history's most deadly diseases. Smallpox had killed more than 500 million people, more than all the world's wars combined. After joining the World Health Organization, Dr. Brilliant was there when the final case of smallpox was removed from the earth—a tremendous feat for all humankind.

As he returned to his roots in Ann Arbor, Dr. Brilliant invited Steve Jobs to walk the streets with him and discuss a new idea. Soon, he had the seed capital to begin his next venture. That new venture eradicated river blindness—a disease caused by parasites that breed near streams and rivers—in millions of people around the world. Three and a half million people have had their sight restored over the past thirty-five years.

In the end, Dr. Brilliant could not have predicted the impact his life would have on others. He followed his instincts, and his journey was not all linear. He took an unconventional path, and in retrospect, he now sees how it all connects. He certainly didn't map the course from the outset. The constant thread, however, was helping others. In that aspect, he remained constant from the very beginning.[150]

"Philosopher Søren Kierkegaard said that life can only be understood backward, but it must be lived forward."[151] For Dr. Larry Brilliant, this certainly was the case.

Purpose guides our behaviors and decisions. It creates an impact beyond oneself. It comes from within, driven by self-motivation.

> Life can only be understood backward, but it must be lived forward.

We all have a purpose, though for some, it may take time to realize what that purpose is. Stay true to yourself. Keep progressing. Energy will follow, and impact, large and small, will come.

As I made my transition from the front lines of business to my current role, I felt like I had run a marathon. I was tired. I began to focus on my purpose—my impact.

It occurred to me that the first twenty-five years of life were focused on learning, the next thirty years were focused on learning and doing and, in the next phase, I would focus on learning and sharing. As it turns out, my own path followed Kierkegaard's course.

My goal wasn't always clear. Working hard, helping to build something, contributing, learning, driving progress, and helping others achieve more all provided satisfaction. But in the end, the satisfaction did not feel complete. Something was missing. That something, as it turned out, was the self-reflection that gave insight on purpose.

> Strong family ties are a window into how we can authentically build trust and empathy with others.

As I look back over the years, it is clear why I made family my number-one priority, even at times of tremendous career demands. Family dinners, time together, listening, connecting, and sharing always were and still are a top priority. The combination of a strong family and having an impact on those around us creates richness in life. Family breathes the oxygen of life into us. Family impacts us as much as we impact our families. Strong family ties are a window into how we can authentically build trust and empathy with others.

Understanding meaning and purpose further explains why I was motivated to give back to the community by helping charities, why my wife and I honored my parents by paying forward the scholarships that were critical in getting me through college, and why employee ownership makes so much sense to me. It explained what drove me to transition into a land of uncertainty. I helped make an impact, but more was to be done. I needed the freedom to pursue a new dream—a dream that broadened the impact I could have on a different scale.

Autonomy releases the bounds of opportunity. My grandfather always said, "If you watch what you spend, you never have to worry about what you make." Realizing there is more to life than material things helps us follow our purpose. It helps balance spending with income and gain the satisfaction that life affords when we know we are making an impact.

> The thread that motivates and energizes us, when we find it, provides clarity, satisfaction, and fulfillment.

I continue my journey by helping others and sharing my experience as I continue to learn. This comes to life through writing, assistance for charities, my role at the University of Michigan in spreading the tenets of Positive Organizational Scholarship, helping advance employee ownership, and doing my best to model Positive Organizational Scholarship in all aspects of my life.

We each have a "why." Sometimes, it takes years and years to discover it, but it is there. For me it is "Enabling Others to Reach Higher." We need to keep looking until we find our "why." The thread that motivates and energizes us, when we find it, provides clarity, satisfaction, and fulfillment. Finding it gives us intrinsic motivation, raising our performance and enhancing the positive influence we bring to the world around us.

Countless people have found meaning in their work. Often-times, they are massively under-resourced; they compete with the best and brightest minds of their time—and win. Long odds can favor the inventive mind. Passion, determi-nation, and meaning drive their work.

Samuel Langley was loaded with credentials—a profes-sor, respected scientist, and "head of the most prominent scientific institution in America." He had substantial govern-mental funding and private backing for his aviation venture. Yet, two entrepreneurs beat him to the punch. Thirty years his junior, they were fascinated by the challenge; so much so that they self-funded their efforts on a shoestring budget.

When the data relied upon by pioneers in the field proved unreliable, the Wright brothers set out to create new methods and ideas that were reliable. They sought an environment that would aid testing in complex conditions. When available hardware solutions did not fit the require-ments, they created their own hardware. They learned from countless iterations, by trial and error.

When the United States Post Office responded to the Wright brothers' inquiry on wind velocity for more than one hundred locations across the country, they chose Kitty Hawk, North Carolina as their testing ground. Using data from a six-foot long, sixteen-inch square homemade wind tunnel, they perfected calculations on aeronautical lift. When no automobile manufacturer responded with an engine that met their specifications, an employee of their bicycle shop built one—cast from aluminum with no spark plugs. Without the benefit of a college education, these entrepreneurs were nevertheless highly intelligent and practical.

It took less than a thousand dollars to get their project off the ground—literally. Meaning and purpose aligned seamlessly with their pursuit of knowledge, and their journey led to an incredibly positive impact. As the Wright brothers themselves said, "The best dividends on the labor invested invariably comes from seeking more knowledge rather than more power."[152]

Meaning and purpose drive us to be our best. The authors of *The Best Teacher in You* interviewed teachers in Ohio who represented the top 1 percent of their profession. The authors wanted to see what made them such great leaders.

In one story, a teacher was not making an impact with children who presented challenges. Her fellow teachers counseled her by saying, "You can't be the key to every door." That bothered her deeply; she resolved to improve—and did so. Not long after, challenging children gravitated to her classroom. She could make a difference with them. She knew all children wanted to learn and kept looking for ways to unlock the door of learning. Her personal meaning and purpose gave light to all children lucky enough to be in her classroom.[153]

When we believe in the capability of others, amazing things happen. The Pygmalion Effect shows that we raise the performance of others by believing in their inherent capabilities. Expectations determine the reality that ultimately unfolds.

Research shows that telling military commanders a group is highly capable raises performance despite the fact that the group was chosen completely at random. The same happens in school systems. Teachers who believe their students are talented get higher performance even though no difference in natural ability exists. In Scott Sonenshein's book *Stretch*, he says, "These expectations are set in implicit, or even explicit, ways: providing more interesting assignments, less oversight and micromanaging, and more frequent discussions of the 'big picture.'"[154]

Helping others realize their potential includes having both high expectations and providing support that helps people achieve their goals. Our personal purpose can lift those around us to heights that otherwise would not have been possible.

> Helping others realize their potential includes having both high expectations and providing support that helps people achieve their goals.

The educators of Arizona State University have taken a different approach to higher education. Arizona State, started as a teacher's college, does not have a huge endowment. The alumni are more limited in their ability to give when compared with other colleges and universities, based on the fields of work they entered. However, their goal is access and success for everyone who is qualified for college. No longer will the student be on their own to succeed. Support systems are implemented to make a difference, enhancing the probability of success. The school created greater access through extensive use of online education, long before COVID-19 made the practice commonplace.

This educational experience is vastly different from my personal experience. It seemed like "sink or swim" was the mantra, thirty or forty years ago. I do not think more than 60 or 70 percent of my freshman residence hall made it to their second year of college. Public universities gave us access to education, but our habits determined if we would succeed. We had one shot—without a safety net. Study, learn, and adjust: those who could do it quickly enough had success. Those who did not fell off that initial path to higher education.

Arizona State University, however, is a leader in changing the game. Several years ago, the university waived tuition for 100 percent of those attending for an MBA. Now they are further refining the low-tuition model. Why? I expect it is because as MBA students achieve future success, how can they turn their back on the ASU development office when it's their turn to help fellow students? I know I wouldn't be able to. Our success comes from those around us. Others have helped make us what we are.

It appears Arizona State is driven by the purpose of making education achievable for all, and it shows in all they do. They understand the impact it has on the students and have created a unique action plan. It is disruptive to the past model of education because leaders lead. They disrupt the status quo and, in the end, they make an impact. Arizona State is doing just that, driven by the purpose of making higher education accessible to all people.

Short phrases that we believe in help focus us on what's important. These words and beliefs should be lived as core values. We need to challenge ourselves and work hard, remembering that it is not just what gets done, but how it gets done. We need to do what is right, not what is easy.

Purpose and meaning in life give us a reason to get up in the morning and make an impact. It puts pep in our step.

My wife and I joined a hundred-fifty others to pack food for Feed My Starving Children. This organization provides nutritious food to NGOs and missionaries around the world. In 2019, they targeted three hundred and sixty-five million meals—one million meals a day.

> It is not just what gets done, but how it gets done. We need to do what is right, not what is easy.

Separating into teams, we were immediately joined in purpose. The motivation to pack as many meals as possible in the span of two hours was tremendous. As we did our job, we naturally improved the process and filled more meals. Cooperation and teamwork came naturally, and each filled box created shared celebration. When the time was complete, our spirits were lifted by the amazing effort and results such a short time could produce. Our group, combined with similar groups the following day, packed enough food to feed more than one hundred children for a year.

Wouldn't it be great if our lives could generate the same type of intrinsic reward? If we connect an individual's purpose to a group's purpose, the alignment generates powerful results. Once purpose is found, great things happen.

Example after example exists of the power of pro-social motivation; doing something for others is so much more powerful than doing it for ourselves.

Adam Grant, a researcher and *New York Times* best-selling author, tested pro-social motivation during his PhD work. He looked to influence students who were raising money for the university. The rejection rate when the study began was 93 percent—a tough job.

He tried a series of methods to gain greater performance but experienced no success until he had a student who benefited from the work speak to the group about the impact it made in her life.

Results spiked by 172 percent. The student fundraisers found more ways they could help students like the speaker. Seeing those who benefited from the work gave purpose to the call center employees, dramatically improving performance.[155]

Hospital-borne infections cause ninety-nine thousand deaths each year. As we all now know, based on the impact of the coronavirus, handwashing hygiene is key to reducing infection. When researchers asked doctors to wash their hands to protect themselves, no change in behavior occurred. However, when signs were posted indicating that hand washing protected the safety of patients, hand washing compliance spiked dramatically. Pro-social motivation is powerful.[156]

Think of a time when you did something for the benefit of someone else. Most likely, your resilience was stronger, you enjoyed the journey, and you achieved the desired result. Once we know pro-social motivation exists, we see it over and over again—in movies, sports, biographies, and in everyday life.

When a group adopts a mission and purpose as their own, amazing things happen. Performance can be raised to a level never before seen. It reveals the untapped potential in all of us that, if triggered, optimizes our own performance and the performance of those around us.

DTE, an energy firm in greater Detroit, has embraced Positive Organizational Scholarship. Though initially they had set the goal to "be the best at what they do in the world," now they have altered the goal to "be the best they can be for the world."[157]

The energy firm sees its impact and knows business can drive changes that impact the lives of those in the community, not just the shareholders. Being good for the community is good for the business. The purpose of the organization catalyzes employees in a common mission.

Purpose drives us. *Forbes* magazine asked the question, *"Could the next Steve Jobs be a Black woman?"* The woman they were addressing has focused on improving the financial acumen of those lacking the benefit of higher education. She began her mission at the age of six.

In spite of being consistently underestimated based on her gender, race, age, and yes, even height, Angel Rich created Credit Slacker in 2013. Intuitively, Angel lives a life of meaning and purpose. She had clarity in her personal values and identified the problem she was looking to solve. She understood the perspective of others. She knew what they faced and how to approach it in a new and interesting way.

Credit Slacker was named the "best learning game in the country" by the Office of First Lady Michelle Obama and "the best solution for reducing poverty" by JP Morgan Chase, among many other awards. Through game simulations, improvement in real-life financial decisions becomes a reality.

Angel's purpose shines through in all that she does. In spite of the odds being stacked against her in the world of venture capital, where merely 4 percent of tech startups are led by African American women, she persevered and received funding. She collaborated with others and drove an action plan to create results—significant results. The app is available in twenty-one languages across sixty different countries and is continuing to make a big impact.[158]

Hope transcends purpose. Researcher Oana Branzei at the University of Western Ontario writes, "Hope is the will to keep searching for something better." Hope's main function is to maintain and sustain action. Hope betters self-confidence, clarity, creativity, work ethic, and productivity. Research shows that suffering does not lead to hopelessness, but hopelessness comes from suffering that cannot be controlled.[159]

Hope is not based on food, shelter, education, safety, or

self-esteem. Hope is independent and renewable. Reminders of hope are all around us, and it can multiply possibilities.[160]

LePepe loved to run, and he ran every chance he could. He was a six-year-old boy growing up in war-torn Sudan. An outdoor church he attended on Sunday morning, which should have been a refuge, became a hunting ground of the militia. All the boys were taken and enslaved, and some died. LePepe, though, was lucky. Older boys became his "angels," and three of them led a late-night escape with LePepe three weeks after his arrival, running barefoot for days through the African bush.

When the boys were discovered, they thought they were going back to horrible conditions. Instead, Kenyan border guards moved them into a refugee camp. Ten years passed. Over those years, they hid their allotment of food from those who were bigger and older than them so it wouldn't get stolen. They also scrounged food from the remains thrown away by United Nations workers each Tuesday evening.

One Sunday morning, hope came in the form of transport out of Africa for 3,500 children held in the refugee camp. Personal essays would determine those lucky enough to go. LePepe wrote his story, and he was one of the lucky ones. LePepe was on his way to a new life outside of war-torn Sudan.

For the first time, LePepe had a bed, indoor plumbing, food, and a new family who loved him like a son. He also finally had shoes in which to run. And run he did—all the way through high school, college, and into the Olympic games.

At the Olympics, a flag bearer is determined for each country. Each sport represented in the Olympics nominates a member of their sport to carry the national flag. One by one, those recommended by the other sports came forward to nominate LePepe—without hesitation or the customary final vote of all the athletes. LePepe became the unlikely future flag bearer at the Olympic Games for his beloved country, the USA. When President George W. Bush met LePepe he said, "make sure the flag doesn't touch the ground." LePepe held the flag high.

LePepe made it from his ravaged life in Sudan to the USA. He lived his fervent hope and dream, having first seen Michael Johnson run in the Olympics on a small television powered by a car battery in Kenya. Ultimately, his dream resulted in his representation of the United States in the Olympics.

Through it all, he never lost hope. He persevered. He found what was right rather than focusing on the wrong with all the challenges he faced. His calling was for a higher purpose—always focused on helping others. In the end, LePepe not only received a college degree, but also formed a foundation focused on helping those in his native Sudan.[161]

When we have purpose and meaning in our lives, it reminds us why we are doing what we do and pushes us forward. It makes us hopeful for a better tomorrow. Those around us who live with purpose lift all of us. They have an energy that is easy to see. Their passion is contagious, and their efforts are so great they inspire us to increase our efforts as well. We want to be near them.

Meaning and purpose are what we seek. Their gravitational pull puts meaning behind all that we do and encourages us to be better.

Chapter 4

IMPACT: PERSPECTIVE

"We are all tied together in a single garment of destiny."
—Martin Luther King Jr.[162]

Perspective is about considering points from the view of others. It requires deep listening, being present, asking thoughtful questions, and responding in a constructive manner—a manner that builds on the conversation rather than draining energy from it. Perspective is aided by gratitude, being thankful for those around us and their perspective, and seeing the possibilities that come from diverse points of view.

The three most powerful words in the English language may very well be, "You are pregnant." As Bob Quinn says, impending motherhood focuses us on another person like nothing else.[163]

Looking at things from another person's point of

view—the "as if" mindset—is a most critical and often missed step in forward progress.[164] We must see things through their lens in order to truly build connections and unify.

This is what perspective is all about. In everything we do, whether in our personal life, with a group, or in our community, others are affected. Sometimes when we seek change, others prefer the status quo and may be slow to shift their mindset. Sometimes, others simply want their voices heard. In all cases, the point of view of others needs to be considered. It needs to be weighed and valued. It provides insight and shapes our collective path forward.

> Paying attention to the cause and effect of our actions allows us to modify behaviors in small ways that generate improved results.

What we do, how we act, and how we interact with others is controlled by each of us, every day. Paying attention to the cause and effect of our actions allows us to modify behaviors in small ways that generate improved results. We need to be mindful of those moves and continue to refine how we act to gain the most natural and productive response from others.

Complexity is everywhere. Breaking it down by understanding the perspective of others gives the opportunity for meaningful, lasting impact. Considering others' perspective becomes contagious, which advances the good of the whole, not just the individual.[165]

This is another key takeaway: We need to consciously and continually seek to understand the perspective of others.

When my father was eighty-five, he suffered an anoxic event—a lack of oxygen to the brain for fifteen minutes—that caused hospitalization, rehab, then memory care, and finally assisted living. During this course of time, his care was complex.

Unfortunately, no doctor acted as the quarterback for his care. The hospital doctors changed daily. The rehab facility doctor spread time across hundreds of patients and only addressed immediate and urgent needs. The internist who served as my father's primary care doctor disengaged, deferring to others.

When urgent changes in prescriptions were needed, I reached out to his internist. After initially indicating he would help, I received a call at the end of the business day saying he would defer to the rehab doctor. I was disappointed. The internist stepped away and did not make recommendations, providing no help. Decades of knowledge about my father and his full medical history drifted away.

> We need to consciously and continually seek to understand the perspective of others.

As time passed and my father moved to an assisted living home, the internist once again became his primary care physician. However, because of his condition, my father was physically unable to go to the doctor's office.

Over time, the internist counseled us toward the benefits of hospice care. This appeared to require yet another change in doctor. After initial frustration, it occurred to me to look at the situation from the internist's point of view. It was not fair to him that he could not see my father in his office. And, like most doctors, he did not make house calls.

With this mental shift, the dialogue changed. As I talked through the next steps with the internist, I moved from being unreceptive to understanding his approach. I told him our concerns about changing to hospice care. We did not want to lose contact with a doctor of his talent and have my father's care put into the hands of an unknown new doctor, but it was not fair to him to continue as his doctor since my father was physically unable to come to the office. Maybe it was time to move on.

Twenty-four hours later I received a call from my mother. The internist had made a house call. He gave my father a full medical evaluation and hugged my mother twice. He said he would be my father's hospice doctor. He passed along his mobile phone number to the owner of the assisted living home and said he would take care of my dad for the rest of his life.

The benefit of his actions went beyond our family. One of the assisted care nurses saw the doctor outside of the office in a social setting a week after his visit and thanked him. He beamed a large smile and said, "I feel like I am practicing medicine again." The visit had renewed him as well as us.

What amazes me about this sequence of events is how blind I was to the doctor's point of view. When we are in the moment, it is hard to pause and consider other perspectives, even when we consciously work to include it throughout our day.

Having perspective does, however, enable progress in

new and different ways. Perspective grows our understanding. It allows us to pivot and adapt. It builds a mosaic of thought that allows us to connect and solve challenges in ways that benefit ourselves and those around us. And, in this case, it brought joy, knowing our dad would have the best medical care possible for the rest of his life.

In early 2020, I took a photography class from a noted *National Geographic* photographer. She knows perspective, both from a photography standpoint and in terms of how it impacts Teamflow.

When photographing children she said, "Enter their world . . . get down on your knees." A photographer of children needs to see the world as children do.

As she travels around the globe, she focuses on "the human—not the costume." After taking an impromptu photo of a person, she approaches them. If they are sitting, she gets down on one knee and drops successively lower and lower to make them comfortable. Taking a submissive posture does just that; she connects with them on a human level. She attempts to see the world as they see it. That element, the human element of her work, makes it stand out. It is authentic. It adds depth and impact. Having the perspective of others permeates each of our lives. We simply need to open ourselves to it.

The third most popular course at Harvard is captured in the book *The Path—What Chinese Philosophers Can Teach Us about the Good Life* by Michael Puett, a professor of Chinese history at Harvard, and Christine Gross-Loh, a Harvard PhD in East Asian history.

Many of us have been taught to "look out for number one." Some parents teach that the world should accept us as we are—the world should come to us, rather than us adapting to the world. In contrast, ancient Chinese philosophers believe we need to adapt to our environment. Chinese philosophers believe that viewing issues "as if" we were on the other side of the conversation provides insight, which allows community gain to be greater than individual gain. Adjusting our behavior by considering the reaction from the other side of our interaction is key to advancement and improvement. This should not be confused with conformity.

Rather, if one is looking to change society—or a much smaller group—for the better, we need to adapt and adjust our behavior to maximize the impact and adoption of change in those around us. We need to note patterns and shift behaviors to draw out the best in others.

> We need to note patterns and shift behaviors to draw out the best in others.

The Way, as defined by Chinese philosophers, is created each moment of our lives through the relationships we form, choices we make, and actions we take. True power comes from creating a world so natural that no one questions it.[166]

I once raised this concept with a friend. He was extremely protective, kind, and considerate of anyone who worked for him. However, he knew he was abrupt and confrontational with anyone who was not in his direct line of responsibility. When I asked him, "Have you ever considered what you sound like to the person on the other end of the conversation?" he responded, "I never thought of it." That was honest. It was also surprising to me. How could he not know how he sounded to the person on the other end of the conversation? How could he not consider the challenges the other person faces and find a way to work with them to achieve both of their goals instead of just demanding action? When someone did not report to him, he thought he would get a quicker response by being abrupt and pulling rank; it does not work that way. When he changed his approach to work collaboratively, things began to improve and his reputation as a team player began to emerge.

The golden rule is often misstated. We typically hear it as "treat others the way that you would want to be treated." Instead, the true golden rule is "treat others as *they* would want to be treated."[167] This is the essence of the "as if" model.

Sometimes we need to analyze the aftermath of negative events, or when attempts fail. Could the outcome have been prevented? What failed? Could the negative situation allow us to learn and grow? Archbishop Desmond Tutu provides insight in the *Book of Joy*:

> When Nelson Mandela went to jail he was young and, you could almost say, bloodthirsty. He was the head of the armed wing of the African National Congress, his party. He spent twenty-seven years in jail, and many

would say, twenty-seven years, oh, what a waste. And I think people are surprised when I say no, the twenty-seven years were necessary. They were necessary to move the dross. The suffering in prison helped him to become more magnanimous, willing to listen to the other side. To discover that the people he regarded as his enemy, they too were human beings who had fears and expectations. And they had been molded by their society. And so without the twenty-seven years I don't think we would have seen the Nelson Mandela with compassion, the magnanimity, the capacity to put himself in the shoes of the other.[168]

Sometimes, it takes time to gain perspective and understanding. Thomas Sugrue, a professor of social and cultural analysis and writer of *Origins of the Urban Crisis: Race and Inequality in Postwar Detroit*, was interviewed on NPR. It is interesting to view his comments through the lens of perspective.

Dr. Sugrue speaks to the core issues that led to the 1967 riots. A hemorrhaging of manufacturing jobs had occurred between 1948 and 1963, with some 130,000 jobs lost to small towns and rural areas offering more land and cheaper labor. This was long before today's level of global competition. High racial segregation, conflict between the white police force and African Americans, including a stop and frisk policy, discriminatory federal housing policies that led to few options for African Americans, the resistance of whites to African Americans moving into their neighborhoods, vandalism, poorer public education, and federal and state governments that put American cities at the bottom of the policy agenda all contributed to separate and unequal opportunity.

President Lyndon Johnson assigned the Kerner Commission the task of analyzing the reasons why 163 uprisings occurred across the country in the summer of 1967. The results were candid and sold millions of copies of the report. President Johnson distanced himself from the findings. A huge gap existed between the narrative of racial progress and the reality of the everyday indignities African Americans faced. The root problem of racial inequality had not been addressed.[169] It later served as a launching pad for additional research by social scientists on what could be done to address the problem.

And yet it continues today. Fifty years after the Kerner Commission released its findings, and after it was followed by many other reports such as *The Harvest of Racism*, minorities continue to face negative bias and discrimination. Powerful essays have been shared in the wake of the tragic death of George Floyd, whose life was taken by a police officer's eight minute, forty-six second kneel on his neck. It is disappointing more progress has not been made. We still do not see things from the perspective of others.

Lori Laken Hutcherson, a Harvard graduate, has lived in the shadow of racial privilege her entire life. In June 2017, a former high school classmate asked her to illustrate the institutionalized indignities that are invisible to those who do not experience them. She decided to respond clearly and honestly.

Hutcherson's sister endured racial slurs for beating a white classmate in a race—in the first grade. Solely because of the Hutchersons' race, assailants threw rocks into the family pool when the sisters were growing up. Too often, issues of vandalism, harassment, and hostility are felt by minorities who move into "nice" neighborhoods. An assumption that minorities have achieved something—like acceptance into an elite college—at the expense of someone else exemplifies racial privilege. Similarly, assumptions that question a person's intelligence, that judge a person based on the color of their skin, or that expect undue gratitude for the opportunity given to a minority, are all too common.

Minority persons, including Hutcherson's husband, face profiling by police and are pulled over on suspicion of wrongful activity. When Hutcherson first met her husband, he had baby wipes and a stuffed animal in the car to characterize him as a caring father when he was pulled over by police on suspicion of drugs or stealing the high-quality car he drove. He had no children. The illusion of fatherhood was suggested by a police officer to help him as he went through unwarranted traffic stops. We can do better. We must do better. We need to correct injustice.

And all of this, Lori Laken Hutcherson says, is just a small glimpse of what she and other minorities endure throughout their lives. Often minorities just "deal with it" and avoid confrontation over offensive statements that those with privilege assume were simply misunderstood by her and others like her. This exemplifies the fact that we need to step into the shoes of others. We need an "as if" mindset.

It is the only way we can truly share the common good, respect, and opportunity as a right, not a privilege.[170]

It is helpful when situations like this are analyzed and brought to light. Had policy makers walked in the shoes of African Americans and had the desire to drive change, there would have been a chance to alter history. Real progress exists based on people truly including others' points of view, then testing and balancing the likely policy impacts on affected communities.

> Real progress exists based on people truly including others' points of view.

Conscious awareness of perspective is where we need to begin. This, at least, gives us a chance. It creates the possibility for creating change that is optimal, rather than under-delivering or seeing significant unintended consequences.

We must be present. We can process six hundred words per minute. Speech is normally one hundred to a hundred and fifty words per minute—no wonder our minds wander. Presence improves our ability to understand the perspective of others.[171]

We achieve the ability to understand the perspective of others through deep listening. Sir Richard Branson, in his book *The Virgin Way*, emphasizes the significance of the lost art of listening.

Branson points out that hearing is not the same as listening. When someone says, "I hear you," that does not mean they are listening to you. He believes in copious note-taking. No one can recall the volume of information each of us take in every day. Systematic note-taking gives us a leg up—it also improves focus, listening, and identifying what has not been said or been omitted.[172]

Active listening allows us to know what drives others. It allows us to anticipate their needs. It allows us to simulate what it would mean to walk in their shoes.[173] Listening, combined with curiosity and warmth, draws the best out of people. It provides deep engagement, leads to better questions, fosters connection, and centers us in the topic at hand. If we listen, those providing input are more open to other options.

To enhance our ability to listen we can paraphrase what has been said, summarize, clarify by asking questions, solicit feedback, and avoid interruption—unless the interruption happens within a creative brainstorming session, in which case the dynamics of simultaneous conversation are exactly the ingredient needed to contribute to and stimulate new ideas.[174]

Sir Winston Churchill once said, "Courage is what it takes to stand up and speak. And, courage is what it takes to sit down and listen."[175] A time and a place exist for each of these. We need to know when we can make more progress by listening rather than speaking.

In the end, we should focus on listening rather than talking, seeking advice rather than promoting ourselves, and inquiring rather than advocating. Listening allows us to solve problems, express empathy, and go deeper on issues.

These acts will improve our ability to take in another perspective, leading to increased ability to find common ground with others.[176]

Personally, I backed into the ability to listen. As it happened, my sight was poor, beginning in the fourth grade when I realized I could not read the chalkboard. I had no interest in glasses and did not get them until years later. So, I listened. I focused. I took detailed notes. I created memory games that allowed me to memorize test questions that were given on an old-fashioned overhead projector—questions I could not see on the screen in the front of the room without being near them—but needed to recall at my seat after finding a reason to walk to the front of the room.

> In the end, we should focus on listening rather than talking, seeking advice rather than promoting ourselves, and inquiring rather than advocating.

I now see benefit from my misguided thoughts on glasses. The error of my ways opened the door to listening for long periods of time. It has given me the benefit of being able to step into other people's shoes more easily than otherwise would have been possible. I received the benefit of learning the value of deep and reflective listening.

Ben Franklin had an insightful approach that is a close relative of listening. That is, ask others for opinions. It breaks down barriers and warms others to engage in active dialogue.[177]

There are two overarching types of responding techniques when we engage with others: constructive and destructive responding.

Active constructive responding allows us to be in the moment, fully engaged. It increases our level of understanding. It begins with deep listening. When another person engages us in conversation or shares news, we achieve deeper insight on what that person is feeling. We build on the emotion they are sharing with thoughtful questions, allowing them to elaborate on the news. We fully engage with others. Being supportive but not reaching for deeper feelings is constructive, but passive.

Destructive responding comes in two forms. Passively destructive responding brushes off the person, not engaging or listening—changing the topic as if it did not really matter or as if one were only partially paying attention. Active destructive responding confronts the person with negative thoughts and opinions—actively demotivating them from moving forward in a positive way.

For example, if someone was just rewarded with more responsibility based on their ability, active constructive responding would draw out how good it makes them feel and why they are so excited for the new challenge. Passive constructive responding would be supportive but not probe deeper with questions. Passive destructive responding would simply ignore the news as unimportant—it may come in the form of being distracted or unengaged, like checking updates on a phone while they are sharing the news. Finally, active destructive responding would shine a light on the negative. Statements like "Whoa! That sounds really hard!" or "Good luck having a personal life with that new job" are examples of active destructive responding.

We have all experienced each of these. A Florida State University study shows that if we engage in active constructive responding three times a day for a week, we will be more satisfied and grateful. Similarly, they found that within four weeks of using active constructive responding, people had stronger relationships with friends and increased feelings of gratitude. The more we can consciously engage in active constructive responding, the better we will feel as individuals, friends, and peers.[178]

Further insight on perspective comes from Bradley Staats, a researcher at the University of North Carolina. Staats did research on turnover at a call center in India. WiPro had turnover of 50 to 70 percent per year. First, they tried enhancing benefits, but saw no change. Then they created a test using three groups: a control group, a group that received an additional hour of training focused on the company, and a group with an additional hour of training focused on the individuals' unique skills, including exercises that highlighted when they performed at their personal best.

Remarkably, the group that focused on individuals' personal attributes had 250 percent less turnover than the control group. Equally remarkable is that the group that had an additional hour of training about the company performed 157 percent worse than the control group. Reading into people's strengths and personalizing the interaction made a tremendous impact on results.[179]

Pausing to think about these results makes us realize

how much power lies in understanding the view of others. If we can engage and personalize understanding, we generate momentum that unifies a group and encourages intrinsic motivation. People take ownership when something truly matters to them and their point of view is considered, even if it is not adopted.[180]

Thoughtful questions lead to the best answers. Merilee Adams, author of *Change Your Questions, Change Your Life: 12 Powerful Tools for Leadership, Coaching, and Life* and founder of the Inquiry Institute, uses a process she calls "Q-Storming." Q-Storming is about finding the right questions; if we don't ask the right questions, we will not get to the right result. Questions lead us to an environment of learning.

In her Q-Storming process, she looks for a group to identify a common goal. Then, she has the group stretch to identify all the facts and assumptions related to that goal. Next, she asks the group to list all questions possible that relate to the facts and assumptions focusing on starting each question with "I" or "We." She goes on to give examples:

> How can we behave so our goal is owned by all? How can I keep open communication channels between me and my direct reports? What can we do to keep asking

> People take ownership when something truly matters to them and their point of view is considered, even if it is not adopted.

the right kind of learning questions? What can we do to keep from being judgmental? How can we identify and capitalize on the strengths of each team member?[181]

The Q-Storming process opens minds to possibility. It moves us from believing we know the answer to considering what a better answer might be. It leads to the formulation of plans that are inclusive and thoughtful. It leads to positive impact.

We also need humility to ask questions. Bradley Owens, a researcher at Brigham Young University, has researched humility—a key component in lifting our success and the success of those around us. Humility moves us toward a growth mindset and improves performance. With the right mindset, we learn from our failings and mistakes.

Humility is well regarded by others when displayed by the leader of a group.

> Humility moves us toward a growth mindset and improves performance.

Leaders asking questions that inform a better decision or validate their assumptions lead to greater engagement and job satisfaction of those around them. Research by Irina Cojuharenco at the University of Surrey validates this and points to the value of this approach over attempting to maintain an illusion of knowledge. In a series of studies she has conducted, asking questions does not reduce the view others have of the leader's competence. Rather, people respect a leader who seeks alternative views and listens to the point of view of others. This kind of intellectual humility raises performance without reducing the credibility of the leader. It models behavior that cascades through an entire group, lifting performance as a whole.[182]

As we interact with others, we sometimes need to bring bad news forward. When we do, we must put ourselves in their shoes. We need to be in the right internal state, use compassionate phrases, have empathy, use metaphors, express deep understanding, and show mutual compassion. It should be done as soon as realistically possible with awareness of the lens through which the recipient will view it.

Perspective can also alter the results of interactions with strangers. For example, researchers in Boston went into a train station and asked to use people's cell phones. As you can imagine, the rejection rate was high. Then, they altered the way they made the request. "The weather outside is awful, may I use your cell phone?" More than four times as many people, specifically 422 percent more, allowed the Harvard researchers to use their cell phones with the altered approach. Making a personal connection is powerful.[183]

When sharing this research with a group of executives, one executive said, "So, if we start a brief personal conversation with our clients before getting into the details of a repair, we might gain both a stronger bond with the client and more understanding of the time it takes to make the repair?" Exactly. Taking a moment to engage someone and hear a perspective from them builds high quality connections, trust, cooperation, and flexibility. A small investment in a relationship pays high dividends.

It is not always easy to be patient and accept the perspective of a group of people. I once met with a group of employees that were about to become 100 percent employee owners of their firm. As a result, the employees were taking no risk. No financial commitment or personal liability was being asked of any of them. If the ESOP failed, the stock would revert to the three previous owners, who were financing the transaction.

> A small investment in a relationship pays high dividends.

Why, then, was there so much resistance in the room? After a long discussion, consensus was reached to go forward with the transition to employee ownership. During this time, each hesitation allowed insight into their point of view. Addressing their concerns led to understanding and agreement. Inasmuch as it would have been easier to declare, "Do it! This is one of the best workdays of your life!", it is far better to listen and understand. Telling is not as impactful as creating mutual agreement.

Even when a tremendous upside exists and the downside is the status quo, resistance to change persists. Generally, we prefer the status quo. Sometimes, however, it is important to know the status quo is temporary. It will not last forever. In this case, one of the owners had already retired, one was nearing retirement, and the third owner was not far behind. If the employees said no, other options needed to be considered for the business. Delaying change to a "better time" is not always an option. A perfect time never exists.

Understanding the perspective of the employees and their lack of in-depth knowledge about the transition was key in making an impact for each of them.

A minister once told me how surprised he was at what his parishioners heard versus what he said. We each understand what others say through the lens of our unique life experiences. In order to truly understand the perspective of others, we need to ask questions and listen for cues that help us enable our collective goals.

Perspective is conveyed in how we treat others. Gratitude seems, at first blush, to be soft. According to the Greater Good Science Center in Berkeley, California, only 10 percent of Americans express gratitude to colleagues daily. Fully 50 to 60 percent of Americans rarely or never express gratitude. No wonder we appreciate it so much when someone is genuinely grateful. Perspective enables gratefulness.[184]

Being grateful improves sleep—by a full thirty minutes per night. Gratitude creates a greater feeling of trust and patience. Robert Emmons, a researcher on gratitude at UC Davis says, "Gratitude promotes innovative thinking, flexibility, openness, curiosity, and the love of learning."

Gratitude also leads to higher levels of positive emotions, improved relationships, feeling more loving and forgiving, increased ability to deal with stress, greater physical health, more optimism, and feeling better about life as a whole.[185]

Cardiac patients who blamed their heart attack on others were eight times more likely to have another heart attack within five years. Patients who were grateful for a second chance at life and accepted responsibility for poor life choices had a reduced risk for subsequent heart attacks.[186]

Science has proven that the chemical bond—the actual chemistry of the brain—between two individuals measurably changes when genuine gratitude is expressed to another individual. Being grateful not only increases our own happiness, but also the happiness of those around us. It is contagious.[187] And the norm of reciprocity guides our behavior. We get what we give. If we treat others well, others will "pay it forward" and treat those around them in the same manner.[188]

> Being grateful not only increases our own happiness, but also the happiness of those around us.

We had furniture being delivered to a condominium we owned in Ann Arbor, Michigan. The team delivering it was running early and called to inform us. We were ten minutes behind them, but still on time. As the delivery team started unloading, the manager of the complex became visibly irritable. He launched a verbal assault as we arrived. Not "Good morning." Not "I am glad you are here." Instead, it was "I've been trying to reach you! No one told me about a delivery today!" followed by more harsh words. My wife clarified, gently, that she had sent him an email informing him the delivery was going to happen. My reaction was not indicative of my best self. I fought fire with fire and snapped back. Isn't it just our instincts?

If we get gratitude, we give gratitude. If we get attitude, we give attitude right back. If we get pushed around, we push back. Positive Organizational Scholarship guides us toward positivity. Drawing out the best in others is a reflection of ourselves.

As Brené Brown, a researcher at the University of Houston Graduate School of Social Work, recalls hearing from Joan Halifax in her book *Braving the Wilderness*, we need a "strong back, soft front."[189]

It is worth pausing here for a moment. This phrase, "strong back, soft front" captures the essence of Teamflow. Teamflow requires striking a balance. We need to have the "strong back" of courage to follow our moral compass and make tough choices. This needs to be balanced to show care and concern for others. This balance isn't always easy. Gratitude is one the elements that gives us the "soft front" we need to allow people to be their best.

So, how do we change? How do we become more grateful? I hesitated for a year in starting a gratitude journal. I knew the research supported it, yet I hesitated to believe it. When I finally tried it, I realized it works. Everyone should consider a gratitude journal. It effectively rewires the brain, brightens our thoughts, and increases our mental flexibility and alertness. Martin Seligman, a pioneer of positive psychology, has conducted tests that show as little as three entries a day for a week can lift our spirits for six full months.

Research has shown that using a gratitude journal for ninety days after losing a spouse reduces depression from the norm of 30 percent to near zero.[190]

The best ways to think about gratitude in a journal are to express deep feelings—feelings of joy and what we cherish. Jane Dutton and Adam Grant have done research that shows confidence will rise when expressions of gratitude focus on our contributions—how we make a difference. Counting our blessings lifts us up with good feelings. Christopher White, LEO intermittent lecturer at the University of Michigan and consultant on creating positive organizations, notes adding the reason why to our grateful thoughts allows us to more frequently replicate positive emotions.[191]

The power of gratitude in fueling motivation is amazing. Not long ago, I was working on a large, complex project with hundreds of stakeholders. The effort was substantial. Creating a solution while considering widely varied input and succinctly communicating was difficult, to say the least. Several of my colleagues recognized my significant effort and thanked me.

One colleague sent me a note that read: "Thank you for your thoughtful and persuasive presentation . . . your selfless contribution to our effort has been both impressive and invaluable. I am proud to be your colleague."

It is easy to imagine how I felt after getting that note. I continued putting forth 110 percent effort, culminating in an outcome that was successful for all parties involved. Imagine the impact kind, authentic words of gratitude can have on those around us. Words of gratitude move us toward being our best selves.

Conscious acts of kindness raise our positive emotions when we recognize the perspective of others. Sonja Lyubomirsky, a researcher at UC Riverside, found that happiness is boosted for months after performing five small acts or one large act of kindness in as little as a single day.[192]

> Viewing life though a positive lens can help turn adversity into triumph, failure into future success, and feelings of helplessness into a motivator for positive change.

Writing a letter of gratitude to those who have helped us has a huge impact on both the recipient and the writer. These unexpected moments lift others up.[193] Imagine receiving a note from someone you helped, thanking you for how you made an impact on their life; handwritten thank-you notes are a powerful means of expressing gratitude. Research shows "note writers feel significantly less depressed and the gratitude afterglow stays with them for a month."[194]

Researchers Adam Grant and Francisco Gino did a study on gratitude where a group of people were asked to help a fictitious student on a cover letter they had written for a job. Half of the advisors received letters of gratitude and half received a neutral letter. Twice as many of those who received a letter of gratitude agreed to help a second student in a similar way versus those who received the neutral letter. This was a very simple example of how gratitude pays itself forward. It influences our behavior with others in the future.[195]

Gratitude is choice. Challenges in life happen, and viewing life though a positive lens can help turn adversity into triumph, failure into future success, and feelings of helplessness into a motivator for positive change. Gratitude can be a powerful factor in paying it forward.

In high school, my path was scripted. I was going to attend a local community college, followed by a four-year university to finish my education. However, it just did not feel right. I wanted the autonomy and experience of a four-year university from the beginning.

The dean of Michigan State's business school said the undergraduate program in my desired specialty was the best in the state, and I believed him, so I set my sights there. As the thought of Michigan State evolved in my mind, the tremendous financial gap became clear. I needed to self-fund my education.

For the first time ever, I called my father at work. The bullpen of engineers and draftsmen did not lend itself to interruption. Work was work. Only an emergency would lead to a call. On the call, I shared my decision to go to Michigan State, and instead of hearing hesitation and concern, my dad simply said, "I am behind you all the way."

I applied for scholarship after scholarship. The Whirlpool Scholarship was the big one, $5,000. It would have made all the difference in the world—but I didn't get it. I kept applying to different scholarships. Finally, the Kiwanis Club granted me a one-time, $750 scholarship. I felt like I had won the lottery; I was so grateful.

At the end of my freshman year, I sent my grades and a note of thanks to the donor who funded the scholarship. To my surprise, the scholarship was renewed that year, and after a letter of gratitude each year thereafter, for all four years. The scholarship, supplemented by jobs, allowed me to self-fund my education.

In the years that followed, my wife and I wanted to pay forward what the Kiwanis Club had done for me. In 2004, we endowed a scholarship at the Berrien Community Foundation, honoring my father and mother for their belief in the opportunities education creates.

This transcendence—enhancing the opportunity to bring out the best in others—makes a tremendous difference. It adds a depth to life like nothing else. It helps us, and it helps the person we are helping. It puts into action our personal purpose. At its core, transcendence is fueled by gratitude.

Taking the time to recognize others is also incredibly valuable. The Kalb family had a tradition: Every evening at dinner, each family member would share something about their day, beginning with the youngest child and ending with Mr. Kalb.

On one particular night, the children knew their father was particularly anxious to share his story, and his children eagerly hung onto every word. Mr. Kalb was on the front lines of his company, a truck driver. Some time ago, when he delivered a package to a small local client, he learned the company was not happy with their existing overnight shipping company. Mr. Kalb suggested they try the expediting service his company offered.

Mr. Kalb never received calls from the company's president. But on this day, he not only received a call from the president, but the entire company was on the phone line to receive the news that a multi-million-dollar contract had just been signed between Mr. Kalb's client and his company. As it turned out, the small client was a local office of a national company.

> Authentic gratitude creates a bond that cannot be seen or measured, but drives results.

Mr. Kalb was called in gratitude. He declined an offer to move into sales for the company and remained a truck driver for the following twenty-five years. But that short call resonated with him for decades. It also resonated with his children, who recall the day as clearly as their father.[196]

Gratitude makes lasting impressions. Authentic gratitude creates a bond that cannot be seen or measured, but drives results all the same.

Taking the perspective of others can impact life in ways we never imagined. In 1978, President Jimmy Carter wanted to advance peace in the Middle East. For thirteen days at Camp David, he met with the prime ministers of both Israel and Egypt. Progress was slow, as each relived the atrocities of four wars that had occurred over the preceding thirty years. Near the end of negotiations, Menachem Begin of Israel took a hardline stance.

Anwar Sadat, prime minister of Egypt, made concessions

beyond what his delegation deemed advisable. Sadat's foreign minister resigned and returned to Egypt. Sadat's safety became a significant concern. He asked to be transported to Washington, DC so he could return to Egypt. When President Carter approached him about continuing the dialogue, he lashed out in an angry confrontation, finally agreeing to one last meeting to see if agreement was possible. Approaching this meeting, Begin was equally angry, wanting the two remaining issues to close without negotiation.

President Carter's assistant brought forward a request from Begin that came before the summit had begun. In that request, Begin asked that all three leaders sign photographs as a remembrance of the peace accord—a gift Begin would give to each of his eight grandchildren. The assistant, unbeknownst to anyone, then researched and found the names of each of Begin's grandchildren.

> We need to accurately assess our own perspective, framing and reframing it to include the perspective of others.

President Carter returned to Begin's cabin. Though hesitant, Begin let him in. President Carter had individualized photographs of the three leaders for all eight of Begin's grandchildren, signing them, "with love." As the prime minister read each of his grandchildren's names aloud, tears formed. Soon after the leaders met once more, and this time, they closed the peace accord.[197]

An authentic human connection is critical. Most times, our ideas need to be continuously adapted. New information needs to be considered, the idea needs to be refined, and next steps need to be modified. Honing our ideas is a natural part of the process. Incorporating others' points of view makes for a better overall solution. The constant theme in all of this is perspective. We need to accurately assess our own perspective, framing and reframing it to include the perspective of others.

Chapter 5

IMPACT: ACTION

"People don't resist change. People resist being changed."
—David Cooperrider, founder of Appreciative Inquiry[198]

How many times have we sought change only to find ourselves left with the status quo? Knowing the components of change allows us to develop strategies to make change not only possible, but long-lasting. Understanding the underpinnings of change is critical to achieving Teamflow.

Successful change includes finding areas of common agreement, noting the benefits of the change, pointing out what will not change, identifying challenges that exist with the status quo, showing evidence of success, making public pronouncements, seeing leaders make sacrifices, and celebrating wins along the way. We all have the power to make an impact.

No one wants to be changed. When was the last time someone told us to do something? Did we do it? If so, were we happy about it? Whether we want to change our eating habits, exercise regimen, sleep pattern, group purpose, approach to others, empowerment plan, or creativity, we need to personally buy into it in order to enable it.

Appreciative Inquiry begins with the knowledge that asking questions can create a unique, powerful solution when viewed through a positive lens. What went well? What made it a great experience? It aims to discover the best in what we do, dream of what might be, design what it should be, and create our own destiny. We need to find excellence, amplify it, and imbed it.

Many times, the way to progress has been solved in some form by someone else. It is possible the solution was applied in a situation other than our own. Ideas can be extended and replicated from adjacent domains. Once we find strength, we need to broaden and build it.

> Sharing success stories empowers others to translate those successes, adapt them, and provide new solutions.

This is the foundation of Appreciative Inquiry.[199] Sharing success stories empowers others to translate those successes, adapt them, and provide new solutions. If we study and apply parallel applications, we can learn. Change, when tied to a larger plan, helps people understand the "why" instead of just the "what."[200]

Mary Lippitt and Delores Ambrose created a model for change which was later adapted and enhanced by Timothy Knoster. It included making a compelling case for change; providing a vision, clearly communicated; gaining consensus; defining the skills needed, gaps that existed, and necessary training; designing incentives, key performance indicators, and feedback loops; having adequate resources; and having a detailed action plan.[201]

The absence of any one of these elements derails change. If we think about the bell curve of change adopters, some will be on the leading edge, some will be laggards, and the majority will be in the middle. Capitalizing on the early adopters and moving those in the center is critical for evolution. Laggards will come along eventually but will provide the vast majority of the noise that happens during change.

All the components need to be viewed like a chord on the piano—all the necessary keys need to be held down simultaneously.[202] Vision, skills, incentives, resources, and action all need to exist in concert with one another, or change will fall short.

To this model, Positive Organizational Scholarship adds "What is in it for us?"[203] If others see what is in it for them, they will more enthusiastically take up the charge of a new idea.

We are all taught to think about ourselves. Reframing the "What's in it for me?" paradigm to "What's in it for us?" is foundational to Teamflow. Subordinating our personal good to the collective good drives higher team performance and, as a result, leads to a higher level of group and personal success. We need to be thinking of "we," not just "me."[204]

We must look inward before looking outward. Bob Quinn's work in *Deep Change* provides insight. We must be aware of the "unconscious map" within ourselves: our past behavioral map. Awareness is key to changing it. We must engage in active listening, empower others, and trust the process as we emerge through self-discovery and self-realization. We need to be adaptable and connect to a sense of purpose.

Watching for the "unconscious map" within each of us is vital. We must be open to new ideas, new approaches that can unlock new solutions. A new "mental map" can break through when our past mental map falls short of creating the desired progress toward a goal.[205]

Creativity—being "externally open," as Quinn describes it—is necessary to overcoming the resistance many of us face as things change. Resistance comes in many forms. Organizational silos, peers with a different point of view, team members who want the status quo, lack of time to focus on the issue, economic realities that pull on the group, a crisis that needs to be dealt with, the mindset of "we tried that, it didn't work" or "we've always done it that way," black holes that slow momentum, and egocentric individuals who are not interested beyond their personal needs are all part of this resistance.[206]

Quinn explains the sequence of change in the following way. Initialization can be exhausting. Uncertainty follows and is often accompanied by a feeling of panic. Transformation happens and can trigger the illusion of lasting success. Then, routinization sets in, stagnation occurs, something in the environment changes, and the cycle begins anew.[207]

This cycle has been apparent with COVID-19. Recognizing a pandemic existed was exhausting. Uncertainty and varied opinions on the best way forward balancing public health, individual rights, and the economy caused strain. As masks, hygiene, social distancing, and testing protocols emerged, an interim routinized state began to take root. Hope for widespread use of a vaccine triggered the illusion of lasting success. Learning from the COVID-19 pandemic experience can hopefully shorten the cycle and better prepare us for public health emergencies in the future.

No matter how we consider change, one thing is certain: change is hard. A detailed action plan is a must. It must not only launch the change but sustain the change over time.

We need to be consciously aware of changing ourselves first when our ideas are not resonating with others. It starts there. At times in my career, I felt everyone else needed to change. "What is wrong with all these people?" I thought on more than one occasion. The reality was this: I needed to change myself. My approach, attitude, understanding, and knowledge all needed to be checked. When I altered these things, amazing things began to happen. Change in me led to change in others;

> Having the self-awareness we need to change and adapt to the world around us creates the opportunity to make a positive impact.

having the self-awareness we need to change and adapt to the world around us creates the opportunity to make a positive impact.

Beckhard, Harris, and Jacobs created a model for change that is based on the rules of multiplication. That is: dissatisfaction multiplied by vision multiplied by first steps must be greater than resistance. In order to overcome inertia and create momentum that leads to change, others need to have dissatisfaction in order to consider the time and energy it takes to generate it. If the vision of the future in combination with the proper first steps do not exceed the resistance, change stops in its tracks. A factor of zero in any one of these key components leads back to the status quo.[208]

We need to find the key that enables change. In the 1960s, a group of researchers set out to immunize students for tetanus. Students were shown frightening pictures of what tetanus looks like in humans—essentially, the researchers wanted to scare students into getting a vaccination. In the end, this group of students, though concerned, did not get shots with any greater frequency than students who did not see the frightening images.

The key that made the significant difference, as it turns out, was a map. Yes, a simple map to the health center created an impact that was eight times more likely to encourage students to get the vaccine; they did not need to see the consequences of their actions, they just needed to know how to get there. Sometimes, the driver of behavior is not complex. It is, however, often overlooked.[209]

Why is it so hard to be open to new ideas? Is it the effort

needed to facilitate change? Is it being comfortable with the status quo?

Being a lifelong learner is key to unlocking possibilities. A number of years ago, I was in the Czech Republic with my family. The tour guide, sixty-five years old, gave an amazing tour. As we walked from place to place in Old Town, she said, "They can't take what you know away from you." Later in the conversation, she shared that her family had lost all personal possessions to the Nazis. Then, they lost everything to the Communists. When the Velvet Revolution happened, ending communism, all she had was her education, her knowledge. Since the Russian language was no longer in demand, her formal education as a Russian teacher was no longer needed. She leveraged her knowledge of history and the gift of teaching into becoming a tour guide, providing an income for herself and her son that sustained them for more than twenty years.

She was open to change. She was creative in her own way, adapting as needs evolved. Openness creates opportunities, lifts us, and challenges us to be better and to grow.

Wayne Baker, a researcher at the University of Michigan, has developed the Reciprocity Ring activated through the Givitas app. The concept behind the Reciprocity Ring is to connect our collective knowledge, because we inherently want to help one another. Some ask for help, some give help. This is the foundation of the reciprocity ring. When we seek help in achieving a goal, "a well-formulated request satisfies SMART criteria: Specific, Meaningful, Action-oriented, Realistic, and Time-bound."[210]

When we give help and ask for help, we are seen as generous and can gain more supporting resources in what is known as the "law of giving and receiving." Reciprocity works. Though we sometimes are hesitant to ask for help, we need to move past this in order to more quickly achieve progress. When the power of help is activated, the impact is extraordinary.

In one life changing example, a participant in the Reciprocity Ring had a niece who was in need of specialized medical care for surgery on her skull (the bones of the skull had fused too early). In her home country of Romania, finding a specialist who could perform the surgery was extremely difficult. As the issue became known through the Reciprocity Ring, a doctor on the giving end connected the family in need with a pediatric cranial surgeon in France, literally leading to the specialized surgery she needed in order for her brain to develop properly and to live a life without the "high risk of developmental delays, learning problems, blindness, seizures, or even death."[211]

Not all cases are as impactful; some are quite ordinary. Power exists in sharing our needs and asking for help. By the way, "research shows that a face-to-face request is thirty-four times more effective than an email message!"[212] We need to embrace what others know and the connections they have. It can dramatically speed and improve progress.

Sometimes we are trapped in our own thoughts and not open to help. Scott Sonenshein's research at Rice University points out the dichotomy of self-assurance and self-criticism. Too much self-assurance without a healthy dose of self-criticism leads to complacency. We must understand that the status quo is not always the best answer—a better option exists and needs to be pursued. Often the hardest changes to make in a group are changes to those previously implemented "under your watch." It takes humility and discipline to reevaluate what was previously done and look to improve it.[213]

Urgency is the heartbeat of progress. We need to act. We must know when we can no longer wait, when it is time to decide. It is easy to delay until more information is known, but progress does not happen unless we move. Being immersed in a topic gives us insight and the ability to act quickly. Anticipate. Expect. If we know where we want to go, it is much easier to "lock in" and decide on a course of action.

> Urgency is the heartbeat of progress.

The trick is getting others on board with our idea. Sometimes, it calls for making a decision and announcing it. It is far better to bring others along, allowing them to also come to the conclusion that it is the best course of action. This, indeed, takes more time. It is best to guide an open conversation, rather than declare an answer. Even when we know the outcome we desire, gaining others' insight and allowing them to participate in the solution will move the needle far faster than a declaration. It also gives us the opportunity to fine-tune and frame the solution as a composite of the thoughts of the group, improving beyond our initial thoughts.

I have seen this time and time again on issues large and small. Asking questions, actively listening, taking notes, and documenting key thoughts build trust and commitment. They move the needle forward, allowing ownership of the issue and helping to lock in agreement on the urgency—that there are risks of inaction that exceed the risk of action. Once that exists, the team commits. They find satisfaction in doing what it takes to get the job done, reaching the depth of commitment moves to a new level, a level that makes things happen.

A number of years ago, I was at my son's school for parent visiting day. When we were in his sixth-grade science class, I saw a sign on the wall that said, "Some people watch things happen. Some people make things happen. And, some people wonder what happened." It has stuck with me ever since. The sign is correct; we need to make things happen. We need a sense of urgency. We need to make an impact. And it takes the right person to help the team realize and enable what they are capable of.

As we think about change and the attainment of goals, we should think about *when* we act. Daniel Pink (author of *When*) used to believe "Timing is everything," but now believes that "Everything is timing."[214]

Pink describes three quarters of us as morning people and one quarter of us as night owls. For a morning person, performance rises through the morning hours, troughs in the early afternoon, and recovers thereafter. For night owls, performance each day starts with recovery, moves into a trough, and ends with a peak. Knowing the cycle helps us find the best timing for consideration of action. We should avoid trough and recovery periods. Embracing change is much more likely when we feel our best. Variances as great as 20 percent exist in human performance, based on time of day.

When running a project, midpoints are important junctures for the second-half push to finish. Emphasize the mission and remaining tasks if the team is united in a common goal. If they are hesitant and not fully engaged, emphasize the successes to date to create energy in the second half of the project.

Pink points out the "Peak End" rule. The two most important moments in any experience are the peak and the end. Ending on a high note is critical to positive experiences. We tend to remember the event as how it ended, not the individual composite parts. As a result, we need to think about timing whenever we look to change the status quo.

Oddly enough, we can be most creative at moments when we are not at peak performance, such as when we are sleep deprived. This "inspiration paradox" might be explained by left-brained people letting their analytical guard down and allowing the right brain to contemplate creative solutions.[215]

In all of this, we cannot simply focus on positive outcomes. We must consider and plan for the negative as well. Mental contrasting is the method of focusing on the positive aspects of the outcome we seek and, even more importantly, focusing on the most negative aspects as well. As we identify the obstacles, we can formulate strategies to overcome them and improve our odds of success.[216] Then, after full consideration of both the positive and negative, we can determine how and when we proceed, and with whom.

We need to let teams learn from experimentation regardless of the level of success. Dun & Bradstreet created a "Failure Wall" to let employees know it is acceptable to fail and learn from that failure. The failure wall describes the failure and the lessons learned and is signed by the team member who provided the learning experience. Likewise, an "Inspiration Wall" can be an effective way of having groups redefine problems as challenges and feed off the success of others.[217]

> As we identify the obstacles, we can formulate strategies to overcome them and improve our odds of success.

Sometimes positive emotions can be negative and vice versa. Too much positivity begins to wear on us. Likewise, times exist that a negative emotion, like an emphatic response, can trigger a productive response.[218]

I was once in a meeting where someone became so angry he literally threw a calculator at someone on the other side of the table. Though the throw intentionally caused no harm, it was symbolic. We needed to get on the same page for progress to occur. It was time to move on. New thinking was needed. And, yes, soon the logjam was broken. Progress ensued.

The key is consciously becoming aware of what triggers our emotions and developing better ways of responding to those emotions. We can internalize better ways of responding, ask ourselves why we react in the way we do, and improve our ability to react in the productive ways—breaking old patterns. In doing so, we can work to identify the stimuli that trigger emotion, determine how we appraise and process those stimuli and, ultimately, how we respond or would like to respond to particular stimuli.[219]

Positive energy increases our job satisfaction, engagement, physical wellbeing, interpersonal relationships, learning orientation, creativity, and performance.[220] Emotional energy increases confidence, enthusiasm, and initiative. Relational energy grows from strong interpersonal relationships. We need to energize more than de-energize others, keeping a minimum ratio of at least two to one.[221]

Energy givers are high performers. And emotions are contagious—we often mirror others. A Gallup poll indicates only 30 percent of us are engaged at work.[222] Researchers Bob Quinn and Anjan Thakor have termed the state of optimal flow an "off–balance sheet asset." The description is spot on. Employees are accounted as an expense. In describing human resources, some groups refer to employees as assets. We need groups to maximize optimization.[223]

> Creating positive phrases and symbols can help frame a group's culture.

When attempting to make change, words matter. Symbols matter. Creating positive phrases and symbols can help frame a group's culture. When we use stories, symbols, and language that identifies what we care most deeply about, we engage both sides of our brain. Bringing this to life through metaphors is powerful.[224]

Researchers gave a math test to a group of similarly

talented men and women. The women performed 43 percent worse than the men. When the test was repeated with
another group of men and women but was reframed as
a problem-solving test, the gender gap was eliminated.
Words matter.[225]

An Australia-based company took this to heart, renaming
all processes with positive words. Deadlines do not exist in the
company. No one is dying. Instead, timeframes and deliver-
able dates are identified. The word "execution" is not used for
operations. No one is being executed. Across the board, they
looked for words that would reinforce a positive culture.

Symbols, words, and artifacts are powerful. They can
connect practices, norms, principles, values, and beliefs to
meaning and purpose.[226]

We need only look as far as the flag representing a
nation. Symbols are immediately recognizable and pull people together from disparate backgrounds with a common
interest. They also immediately acknowledge a connection
point to which each of us is drawn.

For symbols to be most powerful, they need to have depth
of connection. Think of your favorite college or university.
It is the experience that creates a feeling much greater than
simply its name or reputation. The connection—the memories—are deep. They tap both our hearts and our minds.
Those experiences give the university meaning, endearing it
to thousands of people with similar experiences.

Similarly, the logo of a sports team or the symbol of
a group to which we belong creates a sense of pride and
togetherness. Many groups provide logo merchandise to

build on that common bond. Symbols capture both emotion and experience.

Confucius said, "Hear and forget, see and remember, experience and understand."[227] This speaks to the deep power of experience. Experience leads to understanding. Experiences tap multiple senses and occur over time, creating the depth of connection that make symbols mean so much more than words can communicate.

The portions of the brain that control words and feelings are independent. This is why we have such a hard time putting our feelings into words. Symbols help bridge that gap, allow us to have a feeling that is the complex mix of many hard-to-express words.[228]

> Finding areas of common agreement reduces barriers.

If we find words and symbols that support action as well as remind people of the action's purpose, leading them in an experience that moves them, we will have added a significant advantage as we pull toward success.

Finding areas of common agreement reduces barriers. Many times, significant overlap exists in areas that are easily agreed upon, and acknowledging these areas makes change less combative, less concerning.

Identifying the benefits of change—specifically including the view of others—helps momentum. When the benefits of change are seen and acknowledged, it provides a pathway to bridging remaining gaps.

Identifying what will not change is helpful as well. Sometimes, people believe change is the start of something bigger. If that's the case, be clear. If not, state the objective and why it is not planned beyond the outlined scope.[229]

It is amazing how "owning" a change improves the probability of success. Statistics show that change fails most of the time. With this kind of failure rate, why try? My experience is exactly the opposite. When the person leading a change is part of the team responsible for the decision to change, the probability of success is much higher. In some cases, failure is not an option. Everyone pulls together to get through culture issues, process issues, and other challenges that arise. If the team responsible for success does not "own" the decision up front, it is easy to see why effort would be deprioritized and the attempt would fail.

Sometimes progress needs a deep action and a big bet. Aman Health made a difference in Pakistan. Knowing how poor the ambulance service was in Karachi, Aman Health decided to invest 100 percent of its $100 million funding directly into the effort rather than treating its funding as an endowment with incremental impact.

At first, the effort met resistance. Other ambulance services did not have EMT technicians and were threatened. Over time, however, the other ambulance services saw the impact the new service had on the people of Karachi. Competing ambulance services began to shuttle patients to the new Aman Health ambulance service, giving their patients the urgent care they desperately needed to have the best chance at getting well.

Betting big worked. Future funding came from other sources. Incremental investment simply would not have made the needed impact. With its bold investment, Aman Health created a reliable, EMT staffed ambulance service. Deep change comes from deep within us, evaluating the best means of making an impact.[230]

We should identify small wins and celebrate them. Celebrating progress creates momentum, and "shout outs" reinforce desired behavior and help get others on board. Celebrating progress drives success.

It can also move those around us. I was at a conference where we heard the following story. At a company presentation recognizing an employee in front of 1,300 of her coworkers, the employee's children were invited. The children saw all those people stand and applaud her effort and the difference she was making. In the past, her children had said, "Do you really need to go to work?" After this experience, when she showed hesitation about going to work, her children responded, "You need to go to work!" Her children knew the difference their mom was making in the lives of others.[231]

> Celebrating progress drives success.

When leading, calling attention to those who are succeeding in a new way helps move everyone toward the direction of desired change.

A company in Michigan uses a process called "Ripples of Influence." These "ripples" represent positive impact by team members that are acknowledged by management. Peers and managers hear how the person caused a positive ripple by doing something above and beyond the ordinary; this acknowledgement lifts people up and creates a desire for emulation.

The goal is to create irreversible momentum and institutionalize forward progress. Recognition is a key catalyst in gaining momentum and the acceptance of change.

We get what we measure. As the adage goes, we need to inspect what we expect. It takes an eye on metrics to make sure implemented change stays on track.

Measurement methods should be clear and simple. They must be understandable and owned by the person or persons that are most impacted. It needs to be regular and go through a natural cycle. Communication and information gathering need to lead into the reporting cycle, cascading to all team members who affect the result.[232]

The process is strengthened immeasurably with accountability. If someone publicly reports on results, that person's performance will rise. They will work to drive results, benefiting the entire team.

Often, necessity is the mother of invention. When times are tough, we take action we ordinarily would not take.

When our children were young, we bought them souvenirs whenever we were on vacation. The challenge was that the children did not necessarily want to be on vacation. As happens with most of us, they did not always act the way we hoped when we were out to dinner or when wandering through quaint little shops.

In one of these moments, it became clear we needed a new approach. In an instant, the thought of a point system came to us. If we took our children to their favorite store, a nature store with adorable stuffed animals, they could select a souvenir they wanted. Then, they could earn the souvenir over the course of the next few days—gaining a point (i.e., one dollar) in the morning, afternoon, and evening for good behavior. Sometimes, on especially good days, a bonus point was awarded. Behavior improved immediately.

Connecting behavior and rewards not only helped us as parents, it was good for the children as well. They learned delayed gratification. The souvenirs they purchased on those trips also became lifetime favorite memories for them because they earned them.

We should constantly consider and be open to alternate approaches—ones that may lead to better or faster progress.

During the global financial crisis, something odd was happening at a church in suburban Detroit. The leaders decided to pursue a major building renovation just as Chrysler and General Motors declared bankruptcy. There could not have been a more uncertain—or worse—time for such a venture.

But then the pastor of the church did something remarkable; he made his contribution to the project public, announcing to all church members his family's level of commitment. It was clearly a sacrificial gift, and it inspired others. More than $3 million was raised in the depths of the worst economic setback since the Great Depression. The renovation took place when virtually no other construction was happening.

Visible sacrifice makes a difference. It has a huge impact on strengthening relationships and in moving others to join together in making a positive impact. When things take a turn for the worse, we open our minds to a different way of thinking.

> Visible sacrifice makes a difference.

It goes to show how social support, accountability, and collaboration are key to forward progress. Can we build a coalition? Can we bring people together? If we can get influential people to join our cause, these influencers can help create momentum. When we lean into a social support system, we can increase the odds of achieving our goals.[233]

Menlo Innovations has perfected the art of using visual storytelling to provide real accountability. When a client begins a software project, Menlo breaks the project into logical pieces. Rather than create a spreadsheet with rows and rows of detail, they create puzzle pieces that fit inside a budget—segments of projects are broken into full size pieces of paper, half sheets, and quarter sheets based on their order of magnitude. Then, the client places the pieces inside a frame that represents the size of the budget.

Quickly, decisions are highlighted on what can and cannot be done within a particular budget. Tradeoffs become apparent. Best of all, the client is fully engaged. The digestible pieces of the puzzle make it interesting and facilitate consensus on the priorities and scope of the project.

Progress at Menlo is measured on a big board in an open area of the office. Each project is visually tracked—where progress stands versus where progress should be. It immediately highlights areas that are falling behind and need attention. It also creates public accountability, because each team wants to remain on time and on budget. Since

> Confidence is built, person by person.

they actively participated in the budget process, they own the results.

All of this is done in a culture of safety. Menlo looks to identify mistakes faster, before they grow too large to handle, and to systematically eliminate fear. As Richard Sheridan, one of the owners of Menlo and author of *Joy, Inc.*, says, "We pump fear out of the room." Trust, collaboration, and teamwork are key in all they do. Everyone matters.[234]

Jack Stack, in his book *The Great Game of Business*, has turned business into a game that all can understand. Every employee needs to know the big picture, why they do what they do, and how it benefits their customers.

The employees, in turn, are trusted. They are trusted to meet goals collaboratively set. They are told the truth about the state of the business. Confidence is built, person by person. They accentuate the positive and foster team spirit. Information is considered and education is shared. Desire by employees to know information is embedded in the organization's culture.

Information sharing and trust rule the day. Everyone owns the numbers and can clearly see the results, and open-book management reigns. For those of us schooled in the methods of information exclusion, the paradigm shifts, enabling employees to participate in the growth and development of the organization and employees. In short, this level of trust works and moves groups forward.[235]

A must with any metric is predicting the downside and working to minimize it. If, for instance, open-book management emphasizes certain targets with large economic consequences, behavior can become aberrant. Beyond predicting, monitoring behavior to track employee "progress" can cause unintended harm. Unfortunately, we see this all too often, especially in business.

The reputation of a brand is key to not only personal relationships, but group and organizational relationships as well. Having a pulse on the process, knowing proper internal controls are in place for effective and appropriate implementation, and leading with integrity are essential.

The feedback loop is critically important. Studying the metric from all angles, from each person's perspective, can give insight into creating metrics that are established, accepted, and adopted by others in a way that benefits all.

Making change without authority requires the skill of building a coalition that embraces the change. In part, this requires finding a way for others to adopt the idea and take ownership of it. When change happens without authority, we are truly building a coalition from the ground up.

We know this is hard. Oftentimes, one needs to cede

ownership of the idea to others. This takes time. It also takes a realization that the idea may not be credited to us personally. If, however, it is the right move for the team or organization and goals are aligned, it is far better to step aside and fully support the idea when a person with direct authority and influence begins to own the idea. In time, our recognition will come.

Gerald Davis and Christopher White's viewpoints on facilitating effective change, in their book *Changing your Company from the Inside Out,* can be summarized in ten metrics.[236] We must always strive to:

1. Ensure we define the case for change after identifying the issue is important and benefits will come from action.

2. Study and provide examples of times when similar practices have yielded positive change in other groups.

3. Connect our proposed action with the core values of the group.

4. Ensure the timing of action is right, the right people are involved, and it is supported with the right rationale.

5. Be intently aware of the culture of the group and fit our strategy for action seamlessly into that cultural framework.

6. Embrace others, attracting allies to the process.

7. Be realistic, making sure our proposed action is capable of being adopted and can live beyond the initial push of action.

8. Understand how the change impacts others and the community, noting their perspective as we move toward progress.

9. Create visual images that can foster hope and a vision for success.

10. Utilize technology that can accelerate progress.

Each of us suggests ideas every day; the key is for those ideas to be adopted when they can substantially improve performance. Without authority, one needs to develop and plant ideas that leaders and peers co-own. This, though, is not significantly different from change with authority. It is always better for co-ownership, as it speeds progress and leads to greater action.

Action plans are always unique. No two situations are ever identical. Scott Sonenshein gives the following example in his book, *Stretch*:

Ron Johnson was responsible for the genius bar in an Apple store; he saw a need, followed his intuition, and the results were Apple stores having twice as many sales per square foot as Tiffany's, the second largest sale-per-square-foot retailer.

Then Johnson became the J. C. Penney CEO. He made significant decisions using his intuition once again instead of testing the market. As it turned out, his intuition failed. The customers of J. C. Penney did not want everyday low prices, they wanted to know they made their purchase when it was "on sale."

Johnson did not take the time to understand the consumer and what drove them. He did not pause and consider that every situation has a unique solution. One answer may be perfect in a particular situation and fail in another similar situation. This is what makes business and change so hard. Every time a change needs to be implemented, you cannot copy-paste from another situation. The answers are never clear. Had Johnson paused and considered the perspective of J. C. Penney shoppers, fate may have treated him differently.[237]

Reminding teams of their capabilities and the urgency of the situation leads to action. Coworkers and teammates can be great change agents. They are incredibly resourceful and step up to the challenge when given the ability to do so. They will stretch beyond their comfort zone once they are fully engaged in a safe, trusting environment. Creative solutions emerge and complex problems are solved in innovative ways. Complex tasks in complex environments need a learning-growth mindset.[238]

> Complex tasks in complex environments need a learning-growth mindset.

Progress requires action, and action requires change. Understanding the elements of change creates momentum for the progress we seek.

So many obstacles can get in the way of change—personal doubt, lack of time, cultures that punish change, conflicts of interest, and lack of authority, to name a few. Presenting change can be just as tough; we may be ridiculed, judged as inadequate, or be accused of "making waves." We need to determine who needs to know, when they need to know it, and how to best communicate it.[239]

In the end, we need to model the behavior we seek. We need others to see and experience our positive behavior. We need to have a vision, show why the vision is better than the present, and what's in it for them. We must note signs of success, celebrate progress, ask for help, give help, overcome obstacles, be open to new thoughts, adapt, and communicate, communicate, communicate. We need to authentically connect with gratitude, words, and symbols. We need to give ourselves the best chance at making an impact.

Chapter 6

IMPACT:
COLLABORATION

"The purpose of human life is to serve and show
compassion and the will to help others."
—Albert Schweitzer[240]

Respect, compassion, empathy, and forgiveness are all
central tenets of collaboration. We need to be present
and open, looking to provide an environment of civility.
Proximity aids collaboration. Knowing the constructive
power of both positive and negative feedback, as well as
the dynamics that yield the best results related to each form
of feedback, are central to enhancing collaboration. High
quality connections can be created in remarkably brief
moments. Connections are powerful. Collaboration paves
the way of progress.

The key to collaboration is respect. Respect creates trust. Respect includes listening, being present, and caring about the family and friends of others around us. When we view everyone as important, respect follows. If we don't create mutual respect, we may gain in the short term, but will not win in the long run. We certainly won't maximize the energy each of us can contribute.

Respect is a conscious decision. When we hear a parent speak harshly to a child we think, "If they only could have approached it differently, they would have had a better outcome." Jim Fay thought the same, so he developed the "Love and Logic" methodology with Foster Cline. "Love and Logic" centers itself on respect and following through. Children benefit from hearing logic in a respectful way, coming from a source of unending love. This helps them understand and come to agreement with the parent's direction. It also builds the child's self-esteem and self-worth.[241]

> Respect is a conscious decision.

It is no different in teams, groups, and organizations. The give-and-take of respect creates the type of high quality relationship that provides fulfillment. It provides an environment of collaboration. It has natural derivatives of empathy, compassion, safety, and forgiveness. These provide the foundation for collaboration, which catalyzes trust and moves progress forward.

According to the work of Jane Dutton, a founder of Positive Organizational Scholarship, researcher at the University of Michigan, and author of *Energize Your Workplace*, high quality connections create greater energy and capability for increased action. We need to create a sense of mutual and positive regard for one another so we can help others succeed. Active listening, being present, minimizing power and status differences, and respectfully engaging others creates an enduring bond. Empathy, emotional support, encouragement, recognition, guidance, flexibility, and concern for others' wellbeing strengthen that bond. High quality connections facilitate mutual success, increase our capacity to think and create, raise our physiological health, and lift our adaptability and resilience.[242]

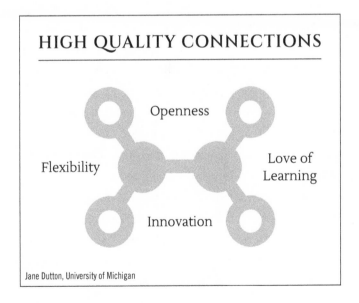

HIGH QUALITY CONNECTIONS

Openness

Flexibility

Love of Learning

Innovation

Jane Dutton, University of Michigan

Building connections includes asking questions, showing interest, and suggesting follow up steps. First questions matter. We should build on prior knowledge to deepen relationships. Even something as simple as having a cell phone in the open between us and someone else lowers our connection. It is better to keep phones completely out of sight. Quick social interactions on topics outside of what we are working on each hour also enhance performance.[243] "If you are at a loss as to what to talk about, try using the FORD guidelines to steer conversation: Family, Occupation, Recreation, and Dreams."[244]

High quality connections rely on trust, valuing those we interact with, investing in the relationship with positive energy, and wanting the relationship to continue into the future. We need to listen. We need to communicate with everyone in a group, not just the group leader, and to balance the time spent speaking with the time spent listening. Above all, we need to make sure we connect, opening our perspective to the perspective of others.[245]

We can do high-quality introductions of one another as well. I was in a first meeting with a group of attorneys when my contact introduced me to each person at the table. The introductions included "the best," "leading expert," "deep experience," "incredibly knowledgeable," and the like. It stood out from every other introduction in similar meetings. They set the stage for deeper conversation.

We can also do "role and soul" introductions.[246] These introductions do not just speak to a person's role but include a personal message of what makes them tick and gives us a glimpse of their persona. When discussing this with a group of leaders, one of them shared that they do a video of all new employees, asking them ten questions and shortening the video to the most relevant five answers. The video is then shared with the entire staff. It gives staff members a point of commonality and connection, facilitating the speed of comfort and acceptance within the group.

Collaboration is also enhanced through the use of "Yes, and." When we use "Yes, and" instead of "Yes, but," we strengthen relationships because we build off of what others are saying rather than potentially triggering negative responses with "but." Improv actors use the "Yes, and" method to grow ideas and create continuity in their work.[247]

Showing respect strengthens connections by being present and listening. Being helpful can be facilitated by giving access to our time, showing empathy, providing support, and having a collective rather than individual mindset. Play can be powerful as well. If we can engage with a smile, we can break down barriers and better our relationships. These pillars allow us to consider ways we can increase our high quality connections.[248]

> High quality connections are the building blocks of enduring relationships.

Personal connections matter. High quality connections are the building blocks of enduring relationships. Knowing others, caring for them, and having empathy for their needs allows for holistic solutions and enables significant progress. We must continuously build high quality connections in all aspects of our lives.

A hospital worker uses a small trick to open conversation with her cancer patients. She cleans rooms daily and often sees new patients that she would like to open a caring relationship with. When she needs an ice-breaker, she intentionally runs her cart into a wall to generate a small laugh. It works. She has found a way to open the door to a high quality connection.

In the end, kindness leads to transcendence. Emphasizing the inclusion of others strengthens bonds. Authentic caring for others creates lasting relationships and fulfillment.[249]

In his book, *The Perfect Plan*, Don Barden discusses the impact of connecting with others when providing professional services in the 401k business. Experience told him facts accounted for 15 percent of a client's decision. Fully 85 percent of the decision was tied to emotion. Ten minutes after a meeting, every single person in the meeting could recall the emotions felt, while only 6 percent could recall the evidence presented.[250]

The neuroscience theory of mind and learning goes even further, showing a five percent basis for reason/logic and 95 percent related to emotional memory. People with damage to the limbic brain—housing emotion, motivation, and long-term memory—have a difficult time making decisions. Emotion is a large part of personal connection and collaboration.[251]

Connections result from the combination of cognitive, emotional, and behavioral actions. Thought, both conscious and unconscious, predisposes the mind; emotions allow us to share feelings with one another; behavior, in the form of respect, helping others complete a task with sincerity, authenticity, genuine purpose, true gratitude, and play, helps build bonds and form high quality connections.

The ability to read body language also contributes to our connection with others. Research by Professor Mehrabian of UCLA showed emotion to be conveyed more than 50 percent in body language, 38 percent in the tone and inflection, and only 7 percent in the words we use. We need to be aware of all cues—words, tone, and body language—when seeking to understand the perspective of others.[252]

Stephen Coyle, author of *The Culture Code*, identifies the pillars of connection as safety, vulnerability, and establishing purpose. Feeling safe is a composite of active listening, mutual respect, courtesy, openness, avoiding interruption, and infusing humor. When we are safe, our body language, the pitch of our voice, our positive energy, and focus all are in tune with our surroundings.[253]

These connections, in turn, give us insight. They are the building blocks for trust and allow unification and forward momentum for a team.[254]

Before the pandemic, when face-to-face meetings were commonplace, many meetings at the University of Michigan's Ross School of Business began with a two-minute opportunity to meet a colleague and share an experience. From silence, the room bursts into the loud hustle and bustle of active conversation. Even a chance to talk for this brief time broke down barriers and primed the room for receptivity of ideas.

This is how we start making high quality connections.

We speak. We listen. We share. We collaborate. We find common ground. We create bonds. Then, together, we solve complex problems and create progress.

It's amazing the impact a personal connection makes. Benjamin Franklin, when facing opinions different than his own, often asked for advice, showed appreciation, or asked to borrow a rare book from someone he disagreed with. This small act of openness allowed a seedling to grow in the relationship. Reaching out through what is called the Franklin Effect is powerful. We need to offer an expression of personal connection. It begins to disarm conflict, allowing us a foundation on which to build together.[255]

Abraham Lincoln would change his thoughts to "I need to get to know that person better" whenever his first instinct was to think, "I don't like that person." Franklin Delano Roosevelt once took two cabinet members to Panama for a three-week trip when a public dispute came to light between them. The two cabinet members came to know and like one another. Collaboration followed.[256]

> When we step into the shoes of others, we gain depth of perspective and facilitate collaboration.

When we listen, we understand. When we step into the shoes of others, we gain depth of perspective and facilitate collaboration. When we adapt our thoughts by incorporating the view of others, we build consensus. When we support those around us, those around us support us.

The pillars of trust are integrity, dependability, and a desire to help others. Integrity matches our words and our actions. Dependability requires honesty and reliability. Helping others is shown in both our desire and our ability to help others.[257]

Trust is the foundation of positive outcomes. If one trusts others, it allows empowerment. Empowerment requires understanding the embedded meaning/purpose, the intended impact, competence to perform, and confidence, as well as enhancing autonomy and choice.[258] Sharing information raises trust, connects us to the vision of the future, and raises performance.[259] We can break complex tasks into smaller, more understandable parts in order to empower others. We can create variety in work and, even if we know the answer, we can ask for input, allowing others to be empowered and co-own the next steps. Empowerment needs to occur in a safe, secure environment. "Trust is fragile."[260] It is hard to build and easy to break.[261]

"Leadership is measured when bad things are happening," said General David Perkins of the US Army Training and Doctrine Command in 2016. This is when "you tap into the deep roots of your inspiration."

He has seen all kinds of leadership get results. Toxic micromanagers get results. However, they tend to get results in situations that are static, not dynamically changing. Repetitive tasks having a long lead time allow this type of management. In these environments, a leader can falsely appear strong.

However, when the situation is dynamic, toxic micro-management leadership fails. Complex challenges need to be met in a learning environment. When the leader leaves the room, the team must be inspired to continue and take it to the next level. Trust is needed throughout the team, and confidence emerges as the team is able to adapt to changing circumstances.

The best leaders "lead from the front and set examples." They have the attributes of expertise, courage, and empathy. They develop others and get results. This creates authenticity and integrity. The army recognizes this and is employing the key tenets of Positive Organizational Scholarship, grading its teams on how well they synchronize with others. Grades focused only on the individual would lead to behavior focused on the self.

When the private on a battlefield lies wounded, they trust their unit. That confidence does not come easily. It comes from a culture that focuses on "we," not one that focuses on "me."[262]

Compassion deepens bonds between peers and between leaders and their team. If a group institutionalizes compassion, deeper engagement happens naturally. How is this possible?

A company in Texas placed compassion as a central tenet of its core values. The leadership team makes compassion a focus of the organization, creating awareness of what is expected, looking for ways to make compassion a reality in everyday life, and acting when compassion is needed. Simply knowing an employee has a family member in the hospital or paying respects at a funeral leads to a compassionate response. A committee of employees continually looks for ways compassion can take shape inside the organization.

Compassion can be deemed an unnecessary "soft skill," but it begets trust and mutual respect. Authentic compassion flows naturally. Consider the following note I received a number of years ago:

> Thank you for the encouragement you provided me. I always knew you "had my back." Whether it was knowing you would support me or ensure a "family-first" philosophy (like when you allowed me to work a flexible schedule during my son's two-month hospital stay—well before flexible schedules even were a thought), you provided that support.

Compassion requires awareness. In the throes of the demands each of us face every day, it is not easy to keep it in the forefront. How do we manage both the day-to-day and address the issues facing other team members? It requires judgment. It requires balance. When we are at our best, we know through active listening and awareness when others need our support. The support we give pays itself back many times over. It deepens relationships and strengthens organizations.

Jane Dutton and Monica Worline, in their book *Awakening Compassion at Work*, describe the power of compassion in elevating performance. The more "tuned in" we are to colleagues needing support, the faster we can act. The speed of our action, the specificity of our response to the situation, having multiple options from which to choose, and being able to monitor any changes in circumstance are key to a compassionate response. The primacy of caring for and understanding our colleagues grows efficiency and organizational performance. Getting our team through challenges and back to their best selves as soon as possible enables the group to perform at its highest performance level.

It takes conscious effort to build regular communication and facilitate awareness. Listening—truly listening—and being present are critical components of the process. The magnitude of compassionate responses could be large or small. It could be simple or complex. It is specifically tailored and is not a one-size-fits-all solution.

> Getting our team through challenges and back to their best selves as soon as possible enables the group to perform at its highest performance level.

We need to include others who should be involved in determining a compassionate response. Depending on the resources needed, it may require awareness of the impact beyond the individual, extending the response based on the group. Effective communication is central in building consensus on both the initial and ongoing response.

If the quality of relationships in the group is high, the culture will emphasize the importance of compassion in the group's mission and ethos. With a culture that includes compassion, individuals will feel a need to support and help one another. Culture drives compassion and connection. The organization or group can support this feeling with new colleagues through sharing stories and highlighting the human fabric that makes the organization or group effective. Leaders need to model the behavior for it to be repeated by others.

All of this grows high-quality connections and relationships. People remember how they were helped in times of need. They respond and reciprocate. They are far more likely to collaborate if they know we care about them as individuals. Compassion is a cornerstone of collaboration.[263]

Compassion also applies to how we view ourselves. Kristen Neff, a researcher at the University of Texas, studies self-compassion. Oftentimes, we are very hard on ourselves. Neff suggests treating ourselves with the same compassion with which we would treat others. Accepting ourselves, flaws and all, helps ease self-criticism. She even suggests that writing a letter to ourselves in the third person can help us realize we may be being too hard on ourselves.[264]

The sister of compassion is empathy. Empathy engages the heart. It is a magnifier. Trust is the soul of collaboration, and empathy is a core component of trust. The *American Heritage College Dictionary* defines empathy as "identification with and understanding another's situation, feelings, and motives."[265] Awareness leads to emotional intelligence, which leads to connections that can activate and facilitate creative solutions.

Remarkably, a University of Michigan study in 2010 showed college students as 40 percent less empathetic than thirty years prior.[266] Clearly, we have a long way to go in terms of shifting our focus to include those around us, rather than simply focusing on individual results.

The absence of empathy creates divisiveness. It leads to a self-centered rather than a collective focus. It erodes unity. If missing, it creates dependence on leadership from position and authority rather than from creating an environment where everyone feels empowered to move the organization or group forward.

Empathy deepens relationships. In times of change, it allows us to collectively engage in problem solving. Deepening the connections between us allows us to see other points of view much more clearly and quickly. It allows us to approach problems in a way that respects all points of view and blends input into the best available solution.

Brené Brown's research indicates empathy as a prime ingredient in truly feeling a part of a group. The challenge is that true empathy requires the understanding of thirty distinct underlying emotions. Translating our own experience with those emotions allows us to be in concert with someone else in their emotion.

Sympathy is different from empathy. Sympathy is feeling for someone else—literally feeling sorry for someone else, but not connecting to their experience. We cannot directly translate our own experience onto others, though we can adapt and relate to others based on those experiences.[267]

In order to enable empathy, we need to embrace vulnerability. When someone opens up, we need to be in the moment and empathize with them. So often, we lose our focus and do not stay present.[268]

Once, I was in a meeting with a dozen leaders. One of the participants shared a truly vulnerable moment, and tears welled up in her eyes. Rather than being present and fully accepting her vulnerability, her boss was busy on her laptop, researching the topic she was discussing. The opportunity to strengthen trust and connection by staying present and accepting the vulnerability with empathy passed. To maximize the impact of a vulnerable moment in creating a stronger bond, we should reciprocate and share a moment of our vulnerability after others share vulnerability with us. Empathy is critical to deep human connection, as is a safe physical, emotional, and psychological environment.

Richard Davidson, a researcher at the University of Wisconsin, and Barbara Fredrickson, a researcher at the University of North Carolina, have shown that our brains can be rewired. In as little as two to six months, generosity, compassion, and kindness can be increased. Health benefits, including lower levels of inflammation and lower blood glucose, follow as well.

In order to help rewire our brains, Fredrickson suggests activating pro-social motivation: doing things that are helpful to others increases our feeling of well-being more than doing things for ourselves. She also suggests noticing and appreciating the details in life. Strengthening relationships has the added benefit of enhancing health. We need to create realistic goals, continue to learn, practice self-compassion, be resilient, and let go of what we cannot control. All these lead to awareness and increased connectivity with others.[269]

In her book, *Love 2.0*, Fredrickson encourages us to use positive emotions to create openness. She has found it more important to use the word "open" rather than "positive." The admonition to "be positive" can inadvertently create a toxic insincerity that is harmful both to us and others. Openness signals our ability to be adaptive and flexible.[270]

Fredrickson's research indicates the essentials for openness as understanding, receptivity, respect, and appreciation. When we have trust, it deepens awareness and loyalty. Warmth, caring, and genuine concern all lead to confidence and strength. We become more attuned to others. We begin to feel a part of something larger than ourselves.[271] As a result, our emotions and actions transcend the relationship. We begin to smile, lean in, nod our heads, and use friendly hand gestures.[272]

Kindness leads to self-transcendence. Self-transcendence leads to high-quality relationships, delivers fulfillment in life, creates connections and innovation, and allows greater discoveries to be made. At the end of Abraham Maslow's career, he determined he was wrong: self-transcendence, not self-actualization, is the highest human state.[273]

Connection is a renewable energy resource that makes us feel good, broadens our perspective, and creates meaningful focus. In an era of constant change, connection is a rock that steadies us, gives us emotional agility, and raises our resilience. Each day, we should look for small moments of warmth, safety, and kindness in order to separate ourselves from a "cocoon of self-absorption and restore others to full humanity."[274]

Zingerman's is a multi-faceted business in Ann Arbor, Michigan that started as Zingerman's Deli. When notables, like US presidents, come to Ann Arbor, a stop at Zingerman's is often a must. Not only is Zingerman's known for incredibly fresh ingredients and the highest quality experience, they take building and embracing relationships very seriously.

> In an era of constant change, connection is a rock that steadies us, gives us emotional agility, and raises our resilience.

When Ari Weinzweig, one of the founders, discusses Zingerman's success, it is clear the principles of high-quality relationships are embedded in the culture. I heard him speak inside one of his restaurants, and though I appreciated his insight on creating a positive culture, the fact he knew every employee and details of their personal lives—be it a dog's name, a sibling's birthday, or a hobby—is what really impressed me. He lives the principles of high-quality connections and it reflects directly in the success of his business.[275]

Safety is a foundation for progress. The owner of a certain steel plant in Detroit calls himself *El Jefe* ("the Boss"), and he grew up in a Mexican community on the southwest side of Detroit. As time passed, an automotive client decided to shut down a plant in his old neighborhood. El Jefe was approached about buying the plant. However, he knew gangs roamed the neighborhood, and employees would not want to come to an unsafe area to work if the issues went unaddressed.

He faced the matter head on. El Jefe arranged a meeting with the leaders of the four local gangs. The leaders had never been in the same place at the same time and were highly suspicious. After several canceled meetings, based on fear of a police raid, the meeting took place with only fifteen minutes' notice.

El Jefe addressed his concern. He needed the neighborhood to be safe, so he asked the gang leaders what they needed. They were unanimous in their response: "Jobs. Medical insurance. Opportunity." El Jefe struck a deal. He would provide jobs, and the gangs would ensure the safety of the plant. The gangs brought eighty guys to work the following day.

The plant excelled. Gang members not only went to work, but some became leaders. In one particular case, a former gang member became responsible for a business unit that crosses eleven states. He is married with a young family, and is now a key executive at the company.

This collaborative approach worked for both the company and the neighborhood it resided in. To ensure a stream of future employees, El Jefe began donating computers to the local school. The computers saw use by the students, their siblings, and, unexpectedly, their parents. This led to providing internet availability in their homes. School performance rose. Opportunities increased. A real, tangible impact was made.

The importance of creating a safe, collaborative environment cannot be overstated. Safety needs to be both physical and psychological. Sometimes, it is far outside of our comfort zone. El Jefe provided a safe environment, one in which everyone could prosper.[276]

Psychologically safe environments allow us to learn from mistakes. Mistakes are hard to handle for the individual making the mistake and those who need to deal with its impact. We are hard on ourselves when we err. Mistakes are remembered as low points in our lives. So, how do we respond to others when mistakes happen? Should we release the burden? How we handle mistakes can strengthen our relationships.

> Safety needs to be both physical and psychological.

When mistakes happen, we need to review the root cause. Was there adequate training? Could it have been prevented? Is a system flawed? How do we correct what has been done and move forward, minimizing the likelihood it will happen again?

Mistakes are an opportunity for learning. Future action from those around us can shift from failure spirals into positive spirals that cascade to others. We need a safe environment to be at our best.[277]

People must know they can misstep and be forgiven for it. Forgiveness is not always easy to do—especially when we pass along responsibility to others. Forgiveness is a derivative of trust and helping others succeed. Embracing the collective good means we trust others and support them by helping them to improve while allowing them the room to learn and grow in the process.

We can all sense safety. If we know we can fail and still succeed, we press forward, taking risks and, ultimately, making a far greater impact than we otherwise would have made.

All of this is considered in terms of trust and support. What would be gained without the spirit of forgiveness? We need to learn and get better together. Together, we can succeed in ways no individual can do alone. Forgiveness helps us grow.

> When forgiveness is woven into the fabric of our philosophy and our actions, we can turn mistakes into learning opportunities and make good things happen.

Forgiveness is not soft. We need to own responsibility with others. Training may be inadequate, but the team member may have great talent, and therefore forgiveness may be the only responsible answer. When forgiveness is woven into the fabric of our philosophy and our actions, we can turn mistakes into learning opportunities and make good things happen. People on the receiving end of forgiveness remember it for a very long time.

The concept of forgiveness does not mean all people are in the right roles. Sometimes, changes need to be made. Forgiveness points to understanding the "why" behind the error. Was it preventable, or are broader changes needed?[278]

Forgiveness can be a quiet, powerful accelerator to individual and group performance by conveying trust and confidence in those around us. This holds true both personally and professionally. Personal affronts outside of the workplace, including those within our families, impact relationships and lives to an even greater degree than those that happen in the workplace. In the workplace, we look to reconcile, but outside of the workplace, it takes initiative to look at relationships through the lens of forgiveness. The other party may not have the experience and knowledge to reconcile and defuse inflammatory situations. Reflecting back on chapter three, taking the perspective of others can be the key in finding a pathway to forgiveness and growing the bonds between people.

Safety needs to provide people the opportunity to escape fear—physical fear and the fear of retribution. Safety, in all forms, allows others to truly be at their best.[279]

Safety also comes in the form in which feedback is given. This is proven: the most powerful feedback comes from the heart. "I am giving you these comments because I have very high expectations and I know that you can reach them."[280] Researchers have found these words drive greater performance in middle school children. It is because we care. They are special. It is because the other individuals are part of a group, because we have high expectations and we show confidence they can achieve them. And, we show belief in the person getting the feedback.[281]

Feedback should be frequent. When giving feedback, we should focus on the person, have a two-way conversation that builds on mutual compassion, ask questions, listen, be specific, use metaphors, show interest in the other person, and mention what has been done well. We should show appreciation, reassure worth, determine the best timing and location, and end on a note for a positive future. We should provide feedback as soon as reasonably possible.[282]

We should personalize the positive because it reinforces and builds on the relationship. When giving negative feedback, we should depersonalize it and make it descriptive, not evaluative. Negative feedback should be about the "why." How is performance compared to a benchmark? Why do we need performance to change to better achieve the desired outcome? We need to avoid triggering the defense mechanisms inherent in negative feedback and guide feedback toward a growth mindset. In sum, negative feedback should be oriented to the problem, not to the person.[283]

Sandwich feedback should be avoided—saying something positive followed by a criticism, which is then followed by a positive closing.[284] We should "aim for candor, avoid brutal honesty." "By aiming for candor—feedback that is smaller, more targeted, less personal, less judgmental and equally impactful—it's easier to maintain a sense of safety and belonging in a group."[285]

Kim Cameron, a founder of the field of Positive Organizational Scholarship, researcher at the University of Michigan, and author of *Practicing Positive Leadership*, notes that feedback needs to allow sufficient time, have clarity on the role and expectations, know who is accountable and how it is reported, and have alignment with values, goals, and the culture of the group. The feedback session should be at least monthly and be non-punitive. It should include any issues, resources, information sharing, training, obstacles, goals, action items, and personal issues that need to be discussed. Mutual problems should be emphasized. The goal is to build the team, learn, and continuously improve.[286]

If we are on the receiving end of criticism, we need to depersonalize the conversation, as hard as that may be. We should label our negative thoughts so they can be compartmentalized. We should not assume our thoughts are the only thoughts that are correct and that the thoughts of others do not matter. We should imagine ourselves from afar and think of prior times similar to the current situation. And most importantly, we should rewrite our own reality with an eye toward interpreting everything with a positive mindset. It is hard. We grow through self-examination and constant learning and modification. We need to adjust and keep trying further adjustments. We should make a conscious decision to interpret everything favorably. We need to develop ourselves, identifying strengths and finding ways for us to grow.[287] Feedback, when given well, can strengthen the bonds of a team in a way that drives optimized performance rather than detracts from it.

> Feedback, when given well, can strengthen the bonds of a team in a way that drives optimized performance rather than detracts from it.

An effective technique used in the medical field for delivering bad news is to ask the other person for their interpretation of the facts. Many times, they have correct instincts on the circumstances and open the conversation. Then, when a doctor confirms their instincts and expands on the details, the person is more receptive to accepting the news. Focus can turn to what can be done in the future to make the best outcome possible. This technique of opening with the perspective of another person followed by confirmation and a focus on the future can be applied to many different aspects of our personal and professional lives.[288]

Culture Code illustrates Joe Maddon's method, the former coach of the Chicago Cubs and avowed oenophile, for handling negative news:

> In his office, Maddon keeps a glass bowl filled with slips of paper, each inscribed with the name of an expensive wine. When a player violates a team rule, Maddon asks them to draw a slip of paper out of the bowl, purchase that wine, and uncork it with their manager. In other words, Maddon links the act of discipline to the act of reconnection.[289]

Though we will likely choose an alternative method than Joe Maddon, we can look for ways that help us reconnect even in times we need to give challenging feedback. We always need an eye toward finding ways to build connection and collaboration.

Being present is key to living a purposeful life. Zen philosophy states there is no past and no future, only the present.[290] Presence requires paying sustained attention to those around us. Presence allows us to align ourselves with something greater than ourselves. Value comes from focusing on an individual and their specific concerns. The quality of the relationship rises when we are present.

Have we ever had someone say "Keep talking, I'm listening" as they actively do something else? It does not work as intended. How do we feel when this happens? Unhappy. Displeased. Maybe even unimportant. None of this is good.[291]

Inasmuch as we all would like to think we can multitask, science says our brains click on and off each moment. Basic functions like driving and other daily routines work for multitasking because the behaviors require very little thinking—until that moment when, in the car, we need to hit the brakes in an instant. In those few seconds, if we are multitasking, it matters.

Research shows that multitasking increases the frequency of errors. It can inhibit our best performance. In fact, for complex tasks, having a place and setting in which we can fully focus improves performance.[292] We need to consciously focus on ensuring we are present to enable the best in us and those around us.

The welfare of others is important. Adam Grant goes into detail on broad characteristics of people in his book *Give and Take*. He defines givers, takers, and those that are a blend. In the broadest sense, givers are those who continually think about others. Takers are focused on themselves. In the case of givers, a focus on others outweighs any personal cost. Givers are kind, compassionate, honest, and sensitive. In the case of takers, a focus on themselves outweighs any personal cost. Takers are often motivated by the extrinsic rewards of wealth, fame, power, or praise; they are more focused on winning by doing better than others and strive to appear as the smartest one in the room.

When looking at the performance of each of these groups, Grant found interesting results. Those who consistently performed the best were "otherish," a blend of both givers and takers. People who relentlessly give, neglecting their own needs, are exhausted and become the lowest performers. Takers perform better than givers but poorer than those who blend both characteristics.

The best blend is having an "awareness of fairness." A person who blends the characteristics to watch for their own wellbeing, while at the same time having an eye for the wellbeing of others, excels. This stands to reason, naturally. Warmth combined with knowledge and leadership brings out the best in people. These people understand that to achieve their goals it is best for an entire group to rise at the same time.

> Interdependence is the true source of strength.

Those who find equilibrium in the characteristics of both givers and takers amplify the capabilities and performance of others. Interdependence is the true source of strength. This replaces conventional American cultural norms, which often posits independence as a sign of strength.[293]

We should all be able to point to people in our lives who live this credo of fairness to self and others. Self-confidence allows them to live this way. Emulating them leads to success, and raising others up raises our own level of success.[294]

When we understand others and work to create cooperative collaborative relationships, progress happens.

When Abraham Lincoln first ran for the Senate, he risked losing the race to an opponent who did not oppose slavery. Even though he was leading the three-way race, he stepped aside and endorsed an opponent who shared his philosophy that all men are truly created equal, even though that opponent was dramatically behind Lincoln. The race was won by the person Lincoln endorsed, and slavery moved one step closer to its end.

Later, Lincoln won a Senate seat. As he made his way to the presidency, he continued listening and learning. He looked at the world through a lens focused on empathy and collaboration, a lens that was grounded in finding a way to end slavery. It was not easy, but he succeeded; his leadership epitomizes the tenets of Teamflow and Positive Organizational Scholarship.

Lincoln had family members serving on both sides of the Civil War. He matured in sorrow and found meaning in the anguish facing the nation. He was never self-righteous, always humble. He was openly vulnerable. He recognized that no perfect answer exists to complex problems. He had no sense of hatred or revenge toward the Confederates. He held a strong moral position and had an amazing ability to learn and grow, knowing there would always remain a tension between mercy and justice. He lived his values, grew relationships, and solved problems.[295]

So, what is holding us back from embracing the concepts of compassion, empathy, and forgiveness? Societal norms, for one, are not helping. David Mayer, a researcher at the University of Michigan, notes that the attributes men apply to themselves have not changed over the last forty years. These attributes include being strong, stoic, competitive, independent, ambitious, and aggressive. Over the same time period, women's scores on masculine identities have gone up.

Traditionally, the characteristics of caring, humility, nurturing, helpfulness, vulnerability, and empathy have been feminine attributes. When asked, 63 percent of men in a worldwide study said society would be better off if men were more like women. Yet men, too often, revel in "toxic masculinity."[296]

We need to minimize incivility and avoid instances of public humiliation. Research shows fully half of us have experienced incivility in the past week, and 98 percent of us have experienced incivility in our lifetime.[297] Incivility lowers compassion, risk taking, energy, and discretionary effort while increasing our propensity for aggression. When faced with incivility, "more than a third [of employees] deliberately decreased the quality of their work . . . two-thirds spent a lot of time avoiding the offender, and about the same number said performance declined."[298]

Western culture values the individual, while many Asian cultures focus on the welfare of the group. In fact, in Japan, a common condition of stress rests on concern for embarrassing others, not with embarrassing oneself. Teamflow is about maximizing our potential and the potential of those around us.[299]

Simultaneously embracing characteristics of compassion, empathy, forgiveness, helpfulness, and humility can be done while also embracing strength, ambition, and success in business. "It isn't binary," Steve Wozniak says to Steve Jobs in the movie of the same name.[300] He is right. We do not have to be abrasive to get things done. We can embrace our common humanity and achieve great things.

Proximity also makes a significant difference in collaboration. Communication frequency has been mapped onto the Allen Curve. When groups are within six to eight meters of one another, collaboration skyrockets. Distances of fifty meters or more are similar to groups who are much further apart. The Allen Curve maps the reality of why face-to-face interaction is so powerful and also points to the challenges of distancing brought on by COVID-19.[301]

> Proximity with one another increases the frequency and quality of our communication.

Proximity with one another increases the frequency and quality of our communication. It helps build a personal bond that transcends our relationships—carrying over into conversations we have over the phone, via video conferencing, and through email. To the extent it is safely possible, we need to have face-to-face communication and strengthen the bonds between us.

Collaboration creates opportunity for impact. It forms a bond that is nurtured and strengthened over time. We need to connect with others, showing compassion, empathy, and respect. It is a basic human need. It propels us and those around us to excel.

Chapter 7

IMPAC<u>T</u>: TEAMFLOW

"Individual commitment to a group effort—that is what
makes a team work, a company work, a civilization work."
—Vince Lombardi[302]

It was hard to find an existing word in the English language to describe the sum of Positive Organizational
Scholarship. This capstone chapter elaborates on the concept of Teamflow and how it all comes together.

Teamwork is good; Teamflow is better. Teamwork is
working together; Teamflow is flowing together based on
the concept of *chi*, maximizing positive impact for the
entire group. At its best, Teamflow is a state of perfect
harmony. Understanding the components allows one to
proactively seek realization of positive deviance, extraordinary performance.

The concept goes beyond teamwork. Why should it be

defined as work? When we love what we do and all pull in unison toward a goal, we are achieving the elements of flow.

Teamflow is the sum of everything described in this book. It is the central ingredient in achieving peak performance—satisfying individual and collective goals simultaneously. We all know when we see it. Knowing the ingredients allows us to recognize it and make it a part of our lives more often. We should strive to enter a state of Teamflow many times in our lives.

Teamflow is when our favorite sports team enters the state of flow. Each member feeds upon the success of others. Everyone is locked in. Each performs the role they are set to play. Collectively, they perform like a symphony. We celebrate the momentum they achieve. We see the natural fluidity in their movements individually and collectively.

Studying the concepts of Teamflow is a great start. Using the concepts to build them into a daily routine is key. The most successful results come when things flow so naturally no one questions the structure. It just feels right.

At first, using the concepts in this book can feel awkward. It is a change for many of us in our mindset.

A number of years ago, I bought dancing lessons for my wife and me. I planned to learn as well as her. She is a natural, moving with grace. For me, dance is awkward (to say the least). As I learned the steps, my awkwardness began to fade—though I was never very good at it. I began to do things without putting in the conscious effort to do so.

It is the same with Teamflow. Once we begin to practice the principles, they become second nature. It becomes part of the fabric of who we are. We engage others with an eye toward their point of view. We live life with meaning and in accordance with our inner self. We approach problems as a challenge. And we achieve results we never thought possible by actively engaging all in the pursuit of a common goal.

Teamflow is based on caring, truth, and perspective. The leader of a group needs an up-close view of all team members. That is, the leader needs to truly care about the people he or she is with. Every person is meaningful. Every person matters. When receiving news that is negative or constructive, each person needs to know the team leader is authentic. Truth comes from the heart. It is meant to enhance, not detract from performance. Teamflow happens by putting things into a broader perspective. We need to realize how the day-to-day activities in our lives fit inside a much bigger picture. This gives us balance and context.

> Every person is meaningful. Every person matters.

Gregg Popovich of the San Antonio Spurs is a master of these techniques. A graduate of the Air Force Academy, he can be harsh and direct—telling the candid truth. Yet, his players know it is coming from an authentic place that strives for continuous improvement. He cares deeply about them personally, and they know it. He provides opportunities for his team to see how basketball can make an impact or put context around how basketball fits into the lives of both players and the fans.

An analyst divided all NBA coaches since 1979 into categories based on statistical performance. He then calculated how many games coaches should have won based on the statistical talent of the players they coach and compared it to the number of games actually won. Gregg Popovich won twice as many games beyond the statistical expectation as any other coach—118 games above expectation, to be exact. He innately understands the dynamics of Teamflow, and it shows.[303] In March 2022, he achieved his record-breaking 1,336th victory.[304]

As we consider what it takes to succeed, the list is daunting. It is no surprise that we fall short often. The key is knowing what makes us our best and moving toward it more frequently.

What if there was a way to propel us to another level? Great athletes have not only talent, discipline, and perseverance, but also innovation. They look at the situation somewhat differently than others.

Wayne Gretzky, the greatest hockey scorer of all time, would never have ranked as the fastest or strongest on the ice. Instead, he innovated by playing behind the net, creating opportunities for his team to score. Innovation is a common thread that binds the best of the best athletes together.[305]

In the same way, Positive Organizational Scholarship gives us innovative insight into the complexity of creating human flourishing. What can we create and embed into our daily lives?

Achieving our potential and the extraordinary potential of a group starts with:

- Creating a sense of hope and possibility that infects each and every one.
- Galvanizing behind a united purpose.
- Realizing even the slightest degree of change can lead to breakthrough outcomes.
- Engaging, feeling alive and connected with trust, modeling passion that powerfully attracts.
- Co-creating harmonic, positive energy.
- Collectively learning in a way that never stops.
- Allowing both individual and collective interests to thrive.

These qualities represent an engine that drives and optimizes performance benefiting individuals, the group, and the surrounding community. It is a combination of hard and soft skills. Teamflow collectively elevates performance.

The results are real and they are achievable for each of us. As we think about Teamflow we look for extraordinary results; it happens more frequently than we imagine.

The lead researcher who created the breakthrough statin drug Lipitor, Roger Newton, is founder of the drug development and research company, Esperion Therapeutics, Inc. and a former executive with Parke Davis. After creating one of the world's most important drugs, bureaucratic power moves drained his motivation. His team of five had grown to thirty over more than fifteen years. It had created twelve compounds in twelve years, by far the most at Parke Davis. Yet, when his arteriosclerosis research team was combined with a mediocre cardiovascular research team, he was sidelined. He needed a change.

During this time, he walked into a Border's bookstore in Ann Arbor, Michigan. As he looked to the sky, he bumped into a stack of books. He reached over to reset the books and saw the words, "Don't let your company kill you." He turned over the book and saw the title, *Deep Change: Discovering the Leader Within*. He read the entire book over the weekend.

After finishing the book, he contacted the author, Bob Quinn, who was quoted quite a few times in the book you are now reading. Quinn is a master at listening. Over a lunch with Newton that lasted two and a half hours, he absorbed every word. In a second meeting, Quinn asked insightful questions. His probing questions helped clarify for Newton what needed to be done.

Deep change is about making changes that are truly impactful. It differs from the change we see in our ordinary lives—change that addresses the incremental aspects of our lives, change that is much smaller. Deep change takes courage. It takes commitment. It represents the big decisions in our life when we follow our own road and do what is in our heart.

Newton left his former position, taking three colleagues with him. They became entrepreneurs and assembled a team of world-class researchers, using the tools of Positive Organizational Scholarship to gain extraordinary performance.

His firm grew and evolved over five years and was sold to Pfizer in 2004 for $1.3 billion.

Unlocking his and his team's strengths allowed Roger Newton to pursue their collective purpose and connect with others who shared a passion for improving their environment. Newton, a nutritional biochemist, and his team of chemists and scientific researchers, shared the passion for translating basic science in a way that meets unmet medical needs.

Newton created the harmony of Teamflow; researchers fell in line behind a mission, time was altered based on the flow of the entire organization, personal agendas were set aside, and common goals energized everyone. Extraordinary results were not just considered, but created. This is what we all seek.[306]

As we consider leveraging the best of our individual strengths leading to personal fulfillment, it can be easier said than done. How do we find our strengths? How do we become our best selves more often?

I did the Reflected Best Self Exercise (RBSE) from the Center for Positive Organizations a few years ago. The results were amazing. In the Reflected Best Self Exercise, the participant asks twenty friends, colleagues, and family members to share three stories of when we were at our best. It is incredibly insightful. A common line can be drawn from the feedback—providing guidance on what makes us our best selves. Once we know what others see in us as our best selves, we are far more likely to achieve it more frequently.

The Reflected Best Self Exercise leads to clarity of

purpose—our Magnetic North. Small things we do in our everyday life impact others. The stories show how impactful these small acts of kindness can be. When we are at our best, we catalyze and magnify the positive. We emanate passion that helps others also become their best selves.

Reciprocity guides our being. It is contagious. It allows both ourselves and the group to excel. We need one another. Success comes from connection, from truth—a caring truth that is meant to enhance and grow a relationship while at the same time reaching a collective goal.

> When we are at our best, we catalyze and magnify the positive.

We need to view life through an alternate lens, the lens of others; remain authentic with everyone's true self, a light that burns from within; listen deeply and be open to feedback; provide help and supportive communication; and be touched with a sense of belonging and compassion.

It isn't easy to see through the eyes of others. Many times, we focus only on ourselves, our needs. This is often as much as we can process. Consciously reminding ourselves to review the root cause of challenges starts with looking at situations from an alternate perspective. Our ideas are good. Collective ideas are better.[307]

We get what we give. The energy we invest in understanding and support almost always pays dividends in one way or another. When things go awry or don't achieve optimal results, we need to look inside and change our view and approach first.[308]

Emotion is powerful. As we saw earlier, it is more powerful than the rational mind. Road rage triggers outrage. Cerebral issues boil at a much slower pace. If we want to be our best, we need to harness the power of emotion.[309]

To put it simply: Good emotion powers progress; too much good emotion dilutes its effect. Bad emotion can derail progress, though bad emotion can, at times, power progress as well.

My wife is a natural golfer. She simply steps up to the ball and hits it. I, on the other hand, am a system-oriented golfer—I need my eight steps, or who knows where the ball will end up? When my wife starts playing below her expected level, she has the innate ability to "get mad" at the ball. And it fixes her stroke. She can channel the focus of bad emotion into a positive result.

> The hardest goals we have achieved are often powered by deep, heartfelt emotion.

Anything we do in life is embedded with emotion. We see it and feel it every day. When we are harnessing the power of emotion, it triggers our desire, our motivation. Knowing we need to capture the power of emotion allows us to be our best selves.

When was the last time you were angered and decided to prove you could achieve something? The hardest goals we have achieved are often powered by deep, heartfelt emotion. We catalyze progress with emotion.

John Beilein, the twelve-year coach of the University of Michigan Wolverines basketball team, knew to talk to his team about what they were doing right, not just focus on what they were doing wrong. It is clear he motivated and optimized his team using the concepts of Teamflow. He looked for generative, life-giving connections with his team. Then in March 2017, he, his wife, staff, and team went through a traumatic experience.

On their way to the Big Ten Tournament in Washington DC, the MD-80 carrying the team attempted to take off in high winds. At 174 m.p.h., the captain pulled back on the yoke. No lift. At 190 m.p.h. and still no lift, the captain aborted the take off and skidded off the Willow Run Airport runway near Detroit, Michigan, through a fence, and into a ditch. Exiting via the emergency exit doors, everyone was shaken, but unharmed. Thankfully, fire did not ensue.

Coach Beilein and counselors talked with and consoled his players. Each player had a choice of whether they would board a second flight early the following morning. No one was asked for an answer that evening. Whatever their individual decisions were would be completely understood.

The entire team showed for the bus ride to Willow Run Airport early the next morning. A second plane, the Detroit Pistons aircraft, took them to the Big Ten Tournament, where the team arrived forty-five minutes before the scheduled start of the first tournament game. Though they had finished tied for only fifth in the Big Ten, the team played four nearly perfect games and won the tournament. They kept that momentum going in the NCAA Tournament, advancing to the Sweet 16. The following year, players on that Willow Run flight led the team to the NCAA championship game.

How did they do it? As I watched the games, it struck me they were following the principles of Teamflow. Their mindset shifted from *Creating a Sense of Hope and Possibility that Infects Each and Every One,* all the way to *Delivering Long Term, Sustainable, Extraordinary, Positive Impact for everyone associated with the team* in such a short amount of time, and with amazing results.

Coach Beilein told me there were no resounding speeches that triggered the success after the flight incident. The team's decision to play galvanized the team. With no police escort, heavy traffic, a late arrival, and only practice uniforms, the team connected like never before. They believed in each other. They had to win—and they did. In the next twenty-three win-or-go-home games after the Willow Run accident, the team had nineteen wins against only four defeats. The team played together. The team played with harmony.

> If we do not talk about the highest level of performance, we will not achieve the highest level of performance.

Creating a foundation is critical to elevate this kind of success. It took years of building the culture, in part, with words. After every practice, the team chanted, "The team! The team! The team! We will be champions!" If we do not talk about the highest level of performance, we will not achieve the highest level of performance.

Coach Beilein knows the value of transparency. In today's world, the truth will be known. We must embrace it. He knows we must express vulnerability to build trust, and he knows empathy grows connection. We cannot ignore the negative. We must look at what can go wrong and plan for it, reframe these as challenges rather than problems, and work to address them to maximize our chances for success.

As Coach Beilein recalled during the 2017 end of season run: "We'd designed and called good plays. Then, the players saw what the coaches saw. They called plays themselves and kept running them." Transcendence happens when we enter a state of flow: Teamflow.[310]

When we are at our best, we create a movement that is unstoppable, transform the ordinary into the extraordinary, make possible what once seemed impossible, and deliver long term, sustainable, extraordinary, positive impact for all.

Greta Thurnburg has done and is still doing this with climate change. She is taking the politics out of the discussion and focusing on the science. The impact of severe weather patterns, rising water levels, and, in the long run, the sustainability of our current lifestyles all hinge on micro movements in the temperatures here on Earth. She is creating awareness and a movement intended on bettering all humankind. It doesn't matter that she is still a teenager. She is enlightening the world to the impact of climate change and wants it to change before irreversible damage is done.[311]

How do you take the worst submarine in the American fleet to first in performance? Captain L. David Marquet did just that. He took command of a sub with a well-known reputation for low performance. The "Leader-Follower" structure on the sub was replaced with a "Leader-Leader" mindset. Captain Marquet changed the culture of ownership: The crew owned problems, so they solved problems. They excelled.

Was it easy? No. Captain Marquet valued each team member. Instead of just asking questions, he went deeper—getting curious with authenticity. He was empathetic. He had a thirst for learning and embedded that thirst in his crew. He focused not just on eliminating mistakes but striving for excellence. He empowered his team with an adage of, "Don't move information to authority, move authority to the information." He created an environment of dignity and mutual respect.

Captain Marquet linked the crew to the meaning, mission, and purpose of their work. He connected to the history and importance of subs and wanted the crew to have pride in their vessel.

Captain Marquet did not just provide solutions. He wanted his team to be able to arrive at the best solution. He provided context and details that enabled his crew to better understand circumstances. He held victory parades—my term, not his—when his team did something noteworthy, such as earning an above-average grade after the first year. He identified strengths. He was open to new thoughts and ideas. He did not want blind obedience.

Captain Marquet built trust, developed his people, and went against the grain on the standard control structure of the US Navy. He intuitively embraced the concepts of Teamflow and lived them.

The results are clear. His sub, the USS *Santa Fe*, was awarded the Arleigh Burke Fleet Trophy for showing the greatest improvement in battle readiness of any sub, ship, or aircraft squadron. Just one year later, the sub was recognized for the highest grade ever recorded for nuclear reactor operations. In the ten years after his departure, the *Santa Fe* won the Battle E award three times as the most combat effective submarine—in addition to the times it won under his command. Executive officers, department heads, and enlisted men developed into leaders far above what is considered the norm.

Captain Marquet found the secret of how to optimize performance.[312] Though the application of concepts differs based on the specifics each of us encounter, the message is the same. The principles of Teamflow can be molded and adapted to optimize the performance of those around us and, in turn, optimize our own potential.

> The principles of Teamflow can be molded and adapted to optimize the performance of those around us and, in turn, optimize our own potential.

The tenets of Teamflow present themselves in business as well. Juan Riboldi is an expert in change management and has consulted for many years. He wrote the book *Path to Ascent* in 2009. Riboldi did a detailed review of significant changes planned by public companies, noting the characteristics of the one-third that experienced successful change, defining what enables it; the themes of Teamflow pervade his work.

Creating an environment of mutual trust, respect, shared purpose, continuous learning, and use of strengths; utilizing intrinsic motivation that creates elements of autonomy/choice; creating a sense of belonging; mastering specific knowledge; and listening, observing, and communicating all lead to continuous improvement and incremental progress. Measuring success with accountability, clear priorities, and specific goals are building blocks of success. The power of authentic gratitude lifts performance. We need to seek feedback in order to keep learning and improving. Stories can capture past and current successes as well as paint the picture of what success looks like. The sum of these factors drives success personally and professionally.[313]

I have entered the highest level of Teamflow a handful of times in my life. Each time, the result was extraordinary. Each time, it took a team flowing in the same direction. The depth that comes from experiencing Teamflow is remarkable. I hope that by recognizing and practicing the tenets of Teamflow often, both with the people you love and those you work with, you too can experience the benefits and rewards of Teamflow.

EPILOGUE

"Research is creating new knowledge."
—Neil Armstrong[314]

Continuous improvement has driven efficiency and productivity gains for decades. "Always on" mobile technology has given us work-life blend, rather than work-life balance. It used to be that market cap, assets, revenue, and number of employees were highly correlated—they no longer are. Outsourcing of major elements of the supply chain is commonplace. The "Uberization" of the economy has taken hold. The "Gig Economy," where freelance labor has replaced long-term corporate employment, continues to employ a greater and greater share of the workforce. Driving product and service cost into low-cost geographies enables competitive advantage. Big data, measured in the sheer quantity of information, speed of change, and variety of data sources, is becoming an "arms race" for business—the first in any sector to master it gains significant competitive advantage. The number of public corporations continue to decline; fully half today of the number that existed twenty years ago. Income disparity continues to rise. In fact, America has greater income disparity than any country in Europe, including Russia.[315]

We are reaching the tipping point. Wringing out more hours and utilizing technology gains to drive improvement in performance no longer provides the sole path to goal achievement. Where do we turn from here?

The University of Michigan Ross School of Business has been studying this for nearly twenty years. The answer lies in the pioneering science of Positive Organizational Scholarship. Tapping the latent productivity within each of us is key, and the result, when executed, is optimizing performance.

Why, then, haven't more of us adopted the concepts of Positive Organizational Scholarship? Time constraints, economic realities, resistance to change, and existing culture can slow adoption. The research is new. Schools, in general, do not teach it. Leaders, having been educated prior to the research being conducted, have not been exposed to it. Blending disciplines is unnatural. It is far easier to wring out efficiency through analysis than it is to tap into and utilize core human science. Philosophy, psychology, and sociology are key to understanding what motivates each of us. We need to tap into the latent power that lies at the heart of optimized performance.

Research shows that 96 percent of leaders are burned out—33 percent describe it as extreme. This leads to micromanaging, less creativity, and less enjoyment of what we are doing. Seventy-one percent of employees are disengaged. More than 80 percent of college students are overwhelmed. When thriving, performance improves, burnout lessens, commitment rises, and satisfaction is higher. We all need ways to thrive.[316]

Certain prerequisites must be present for Teamflow to be possible in a work environment. The basic needs of appropriate working conditions, fair pay, reasonable hours, fair expectations, civility, and respect need to exist. Foundational intrinsic attributes of hard work, desire, initiative, trust, principle-based leadership, skill, and cooperation must be present as well. Finally, the organization needs to be sustainable—providing value that is sustainable.[317]

The sum of these attributes provides the foundation needed for Teamflow to exist and for a group to thrive. In order to provide an opportunity for "Everest Performance," these factors need to be in place.[318] A significant "miss" on any of these attributes could cause failure in the possibilities and levels of achievement of Teamflow.

Achieving Teamflow takes multiple iterations that bounce between all phases of the IMPACT process that has been discussed. It requires discipline and persistence. It, in the end, creates satisfaction, the satisfaction of knowing we make a difference. We can each make an impact. Making it happen is up to each of us.

So how does something that is seemingly so easy turn out to be so incredibly hard? In a sense, Positive Organizational Scholarship centers around our most basic human traits that drive societal harmony. It gets corrupted by individualism, trying to suppress others for one's own benefit, and putting people down rather than lifting them up. We are social beings. We want the best for one another. If we dehumanize groups that differ from us, we begin to drift away from our innate sense. We begin to create conflict and to center on ourselves. We need to be aware of this and fight this downward spiral.

This weaves into what has been called field theory, a discipline that explains relationships with the same complexity as the life of plants and animals in a field or meadow. It is about what we can learn from nature, not extract from it. Interdependence exists in all that lives in a field. In order to achieve long-term sustainability, everything needs to stay in harmony between plants, animals, and the environment.

Field theory doesn't identify winners and losers. It isn't good versus bad, right versus wrong, or necessarily linear. It is multidimensional, interactive, harmonious, and sustainable over the long run.

Applied field theory focuses on common ground being discovered. Relationships are complex and fluid. We look to be enlightened and enabled. It is about transforming and transcending. Measurement is beyond economics.

Time and time again, we experience this. Unless we understand the other side's objectives, we cannot reach the solution that is most effective. Much is discussed about "win, win" agreements. "Win, win" means sustainability. Is it sustainable for all? Can others agree to move forward? Can we live with the agreement? Can we see the agreement living for years to come? Is it aligned for success? Harmonic relationships in any form have these attributes. They continue on in the same way the plants and animals in a field exist in harmony and can flourish.

Relationships can work together for decades upon decades. When it happens, it is amazing. Through good times and bad, the relationship perseveres. It can survive periods of strain and crisis, and perhaps can thrive. To sustain, we need to willingly reach profoundly inside ourselves. And as a result, the relationship strengthens and deepens. It represents the sustainable, multidimensional view that allows the relationship to continue to exist and thrive.

Contrast field theory with what happens when one focuses primarily on oneself. Too often, the relationship begins to fracture. Trust is broken. Harmony ceases. It endangers sustainability and we lose the interdependent characteristics of field theory embedded into the relationship.

In the end, the ideal is to live in sustainable harmony, not to control another person or group. It is about finding common ground: listening, not telling; understanding, not declaring. It is complex and fluid, reflective, considerate, and transparent. Success is multidimensional. We are all interconnected and dependent on one another.[319]

Positive IMPACT is a system that leads to Teamflow. It drives improvement. It allows us to reach our best selves more often. To recap, here are the components:

Positive framing is about getting our A game ready. We need to be in a positive state of mind to be at our best. We affect performance based on how we feel.

Identification has two parts. First is the need to identify our own core values. What is our identity? What are our roots? What traits will we look to uphold when the going gets tough? Second is identifying the goal. Being clear about the future results we seek is critical.

Meaning is essential. It is central. Progress can happen without being attached to purpose. However, purpose is the rocket fuel that propels progress and solutions to complex problems. If others adopt the overarching purpose as their own and translate it to match their personal purpose, it generates fulfillment and growth. Purpose is an independent variable. It is not tied to life's basic needs like food, water, and shelter. Purpose gives us hope. Hope gives us the power to press on, persistently looking for ways to improve our future.

Perspective is the most underused step in problem solving and progress attainment. We must look at challenges from all points of view, even when it is difficult to do so. We may not agree with those alternate views, but we need to be able to catalyze those who hold those views to move progress forward, not sabotage the effort. It takes time to do this. It also takes deep connections with others in order to understand and assess what may hold them back from making the progress we seek.

Action is where the rubber meets the road. The more complex the problem, the more detailed the action plan needs to be.[320] Resistance is common. Painting a picture that the status quo is not the best way forward helps others understand the need for change.[321] Words and symbols can be used to remind people of the progress we seek and point them in the desired direction, reinforcing other aspects of the action plan.[322] Gaining common agreement with others facilitates support. Identifying what will not change reduces fear, and celebrating victories along the way strengthens belief in progress—that together we can win. Being open-minded is critical.[323] We cannot dismiss ideas just because they did not work in the past. Leading the effort with a positive mindset builds confidence in others, regardless of whether we are in the highest authority position or not.

Collaboration requires the basic human traits of compassion, empathy, forgiveness, and providing safety in order to create deep bonds with others. We need to connect. Connections give us insight, the ability to see a problem from someone else's point of view. Collaboration leads to a belief that we can all win. It is not us versus them—it is "we," not "me." Connections give us the social support we need to create progress and can lead to public support as well. When we connect with one another, we are primed for visible personal sacrifice—the kind of sacrifice that is authentic and drives us toward a goal.[324]

Teamflow is where we determine impact. Are we considering the point of view of others? Are we incorporating their thoughts and needs into the flow of our team? Are we gaining buy-in? Are we giving choice and input to all? Are we creating a structure that has the right boundaries in which all can flourish, along with feedback loops that are clear, concise, and readily available? Are we flowing as a team, not just as individuals?

We must see both possibility and reality. We can only create what we can imagine or, as the adage goes, "You cannot be what you cannot see."

We need to believe in ourselves and others, to build each other up and create a fully inclusive environment. We need to transform "hardship into challenge, failure into success, and helplessness into power."[325] We need to see possibility, have a positive lens, learn and grow, and have a positive mindset. We need to celebrate progress.[326]

Achieving Teamflow includes trust, being inclusive of others, gratitude, compassion, empathy, empowering others, providing a safe environment, being interdependent with one another, focusing on collective gains, listening, and mutual success. The positive mindset that drives Teamflow is about magnifying, amplifying, and multiplying what is possible individually and collectively.

> The positive mindset that drives Teamflow is about magnifying, amplifying, and multiplying what is possible individually and collectively.

It is in sharp contrast to a "me" centered model based on control, self-centeredness, and dominance.

The sum of this is not easy. Just listing the areas of consideration takes time. As I researched and noted the myriad of topics covered in this book, most of which have entire books devoted to each topic by world-class scholars, it struck me how valuable it would have been to have a reference guide in my own life as I navigated complex challenges. I have been using the principles of Positive Organizational Scholarship all my life. Once I put the research into the Positive IMPACT model, it helped me order and consider how to make an impact faster and more consistently than ever. I hope it contributes to your ability to do the same.

Making a positive impact is a choice each of us make in every moment of every day. I hope the concepts of Team-flow impact your life as much as they have impacted mine. Godspeed and good luck.

"If your actions inspire others to dream more, learn more, do more, and become more, you are a positive leader."

—John Quincy Adams[327]

NOTES OF APPRECIATION

"Alone we can do so little, together we can do so much."
—Helen Keller[328]

In keeping with the practices of Positive Organizational Scholarship, I offer these notes of appreciation:

To Wayne Baker: Thank you for introducing me to your contacts, for the advice you have given me, and for writing the foreword to this book.

To Mari Kira, Associate Professor of Psychology and faculty member of the Center for Positive Organizations: Thank you for providing an extremely helpful and insightful, friendly review of the manuscript.

To the scholars who had the vision to begin this field of study—Kim Cameron, Jane Dutton, and Robert Quinn: Thank you!

To the 500+ researchers who have grown the field of study into a robust body of knowledge: Thank you!

To the Center for Positive Organizations, Managing Director, Esther Kyte; the faculty that have led the Center over the past six years: Wayne Baker, Gretchen Spreitzer, and Julie Lee Cunningham; long time scholars at the Center: Mari Kira and Amy Young; my fellow Executives in Residence: Roger Newton, Rick Haller, Laurita Thomas, Rich Smalling, and Ron May; long time associates of the Center: Betsy Erwin, Angie Ceely, Stacey Scimeca, and Katie Trevathan: Thank you for living the principles of the research each and every day! **As a further sign of appreciation, all earnings from this book will be donated to the Center for Positive Organizations.**

To Gerald Davis and Christopher White, who started this journey for me by introducing me and inviting me to join the Center: Thank you!

To Roger Newton and John Beilein: Thank you for sharing your stories!

To Dan Drews, Kathy Drews, Joshua Drews, Kathryn Pillischafske, Jim Mallozzi, Lenora Hardy-Foster, Roy Verstraete,

Henry Horbaczewski, Roger Newton, and Ron May: Thank you for the comprehensive review of the manuscript and the scores of helpful ideas you generated.

To Amanda Drews: Thank you for helping me with the launch of my book!

To my literary agent, Lauren Hall, publishing coordinator, Nayla Zylberberg, as well as the balance of the entire Content Capital team including Jack Inguanti and Jordan Knul: Thank you for the outstanding work you did to improve and finalize the manuscript!

To Rich Smalling: Thank you for introducing me to Content Capital!

To my uncle, Gerry Drews: Thank you for intuitively modeling the principles of Teamflow throughout my lifetime.

To my mentors and teachers—too many to name: Thanks to all of you!

Most of all, to my family, Lisa Drews, Joe Drews, Ryan Drews, Joshua Drews, Kathryn Pillischafske, Kejal Shah, Joseph Rinaldi, Angelica Rinaldi, Virginia Drews, and Al Drews, for showing unending love, support, and encouragement to me throughout my life. Thank you!

Finally, I want to share my deepest gratitude to all those that have helped me along my life journey.

RELATED READINGS

24 Life Stories and Lessons from the Say Hey Kid; Willie Mays and John Shea

A Full Life: Reflections at Ninety; Jimmy Carter

Abraham Lincoln, The Spiritual Growth of a Public Man; Abraham Lincoln and Elton Trueblood

All You Have to Do Is Ask; Wayne Baker

Appreciate Inquiry: A Positive Revolution; David Cooperrider

Appreciative Inquiry Handbook: For Leaders of Change; David Cooperrider, Diana Whitney, and Jacqueline Stavros

Awakening Compassion at Work; Monica Worline and Jane Dutton

Bad Blood: Secrets and Lies in a Silicon Valley Startup; John Carreyrou

Becoming; Michelle Obama

Biased; Jennifer L. Eberhardt

Blink; Malcolm Gladwell

Braving the Wilderness: The Quest for True Belonging and the Courage to Stand Alone; Brene Brown

Building the Bridge as You Walk on It: A Guide for Leading Change; Robert Quinn

Changing Your Company from the Inside Out; Gerald Davis and Christopher White

Code of the Extraordinary Mind: 10 Unconventional Laws to Redefine Your Life and Succeed On Your Own Terms; Vishen Lakhiani

David and Goliath; Malcolm Gladwell

Deep Change; Robert Quinn

Drive; Daniel Pink

Energize Your Workplace: How to Create and Sustain High Quality Connections at Work; Jane Dutton

Find Your Why: A Practical Guide for Discovering; Simon Sinek

Give and Take: Why Helping Others Drives Our Success; Adam Grant

Grit: The Power of Passion and Perseverance; Angela Duckworth

Harvard Business Review. Creating Sustainable Performance; Gretchen Spreitzer, Christine Porath

How to be a Positive Leader: Small Actions, Big Impact; Jane Dutton and Gretchen Spreitzer

Joy, Inc: How We Build A Workplace People Love; Richard Sheridan

Leaders Eat Last: Why Some Teams Pull Together and Others Don't; Simon Sinek

Life on Purpose; Victor Strecher

Lift: The Fundamental State of Leadership; Ryan W. Quinn and Robert E. Quinn, et al.

Lincoln; David Herbert Donald

Love 2.0; Barbara Fredrickson

Managed by Markets; Gerald Davis

Mindset: The New Psychology of Success; Carol Dweck

Negotiating Genuinely; Shirli Kopelman

Never Stop Learning; Bradley Staats

Ninety Percent Mental; Bob Tewksbury

Option B: Facing Adversity, Building Resilience, and Finding Joy; Sheryl Sandberg and Adam Grant

Originals; Adam Grant

Practically Positive; Rich Smalling

Practicing Positive Leadership; Kim Cameron

Principles of Life and Work; Ray Dalio

Quiet, The Power of Introverts in a World That Can't Stop Talking; Susan Cain

Running for My Life; Lopez Lomong

Start with Why; Simon Sinek

Steve Jobs; Walter Isaacson

Stretch: Unlock the Power of Lies and Achieve More Than You Ever Imagined; Scott Sonenshein

The Best Teacher in You: How to Accelerate Learning and Change Lives; Robert Quinn, Katherine Heynoski, Mike Thomas, and Gretchen Spreitzer

The Book of Joy; His Holiness the Dalai Lama, Archbishop Desmond Tutu and Douglas Abrams

The Charisma Myth: How Anyone Can Master the Art and Science of Personal Magnetism; Olivia Fox Cabane

The Deep Change Field Guide; Robert Quinn

The Great Game of Business; Jack Stack and Bo Burlington

The Oxford Guide to Positive Organizational Scholarship; Kim Cameron and Gretchen Spreitzer

The Path; Micheal Puett and Chistine Gross-Loh

The Path of Ascent: The Five Principles for Mastering Change; Juan Riboldi

The Perfect Plan; Donald Barden

The Positive Organization: Breaking Free from Conventional Cultures, Constraints and Beliefs; Robert Quinn

The Power of Habit; Charles Duhigg

The Power of Positive Thinking; Norman Vincent Peale

Flow: The Psychology of Optimal Experience; Mihaly Csíkszentmihályi

The Psychology of Passion: A Dualistic Model; Robert Vallerand

The Resilience Factor: 7 Keys to Finding Your Inner Strength and Overcoming Life's Hurdles; Karen Reivich and Andrew Shatte

The Sleep Revolution: Transforming Your Life, One Night at a Time; Arianna Huffington

The Thin Book of Appreciative Inquiry; Sue Annis Hammond

The Tipping Point; Malcolm Gladwell

The Vanishing American Corporation: Gerald Davis

The Virgin Way; Richard Branson

The Wright Brothers; David McCullough

Thinking Fast and Slow; Daniel Kahneman

Time Magazine, 2019 Person of the Year; Charlotte Alter, Suyin Haynes, and Justin Worland

To Sell is Human: The Surprising Trust about Moving Others; Daniel Pink

Turn the Ship Around; L. David Marquet, Captain, US Navy (Retired)

U Thrive; Dan Lerner and Alan Schechter

When; Daniel Pink

Why We Do What We Do; Edward Deci

ABOUT THE AUTHOR

Born in a small town in West Michigan and a first-generation college graduate, David Drews credits his parents with instilling the value of education and the opportunity it provides.

His father always said, "You can achieve whatever you want to achieve, if you put your mind to it." Positive Organizational Scholarship had not been pioneered when Drews' father said it, but he knew the power of positive thinking. Drews often wonders what his father would think if he knew how many times his words went through David's mind during his lifetime. It is amazing to see how true this simple sentence is.

Developing and growing, individually and as a group, is not easy. It becomes easier with vocabulary to describe it, research that verifies it, and experience that modulates how we implement it. That is what Teamflow is all about.

After more than thirty-five years in leadership positions consciously practicing Teamflow, Drews joined the University of Michigan as an Executive in Residence at the Center for Positive Organizations at the Stephen M. Ross School of Business. He found the work of world-class researchers surrounding optimizing business performance fascinating. Synthesizing and restating the research with practical insights from his own experience deeply interests him.

Drews has been fortunate to experience an amazing life journey and hopes you gain as much insight as he has from the research of optimizing performance.

SOURCES

1 Mihály Csíkszentmihályi, *Flow: The Psychology of Optimal Performance* (New York: Harper Collins, 1991).

2 Kim S. Cameron, *Practicing Positive Leadership* (San Francisco: Berrett:Koehler, 2013), Page 119.

3 Wayne Baker, *All You Have to Do Is Ask: How to Master the Most Important Skill for Success* (New York: Random House, 2020), Page 123.

4 Robert E. Quinn, *Deep Change* (San Francisco: Jossey-Bass, 1996), Page 168.

5 Jane E. Dutton, *Energize Your Workplace: How to Create and Sustain High-Quality Connections at Work* (San Francisco: Jossey-Bass, 2003), Pages xv–xix.

6 Csíkszentmihályi, *Flow*.

7 Scott Sonenshein, *Stretch: Unlock the Power of Less—And Achieve More Than You Ever Imagined* (New York: Harper Collins, 2017), Page 143.

8 Malcolm Gladwell, *Blink: The Power of Thinking Without Thinking* (New York: Back Bay Books, 2019), Pages 139–146.

9 Robert E. Quinn, "Turning Organizations Positive" (Workshop, Positive Business Conference, Ann Arbor, MI, May 2017).

10 Baker, *All You Have To Do Is Ask,* Pages 84–85.

11 Charles Duhigg, *The Power of Habit: Why We Do What We Do in Life and Business* (New York: Random House, 2014), Page 113.

12 Jocko Willink and Leif Babin, *Extreme Ownership: How U.S. Navy Seals Lead and Win* (New York: St. Martin's Press, 2017), Pages 8, 30, 31, 49, 100, 255, and 277.

13 Cameron, *Practicing Positive Leadership,* Page 104.

14 Gretchen Spreitzer and Christine Porath, "Creating Sustainable Performance," *Harvard Business Review*, January – February, 2012: Reprint R1201F.

15 In Jane E. Dutton and Gretchen Spreitzer, *How to Be a Positive Leader: Insights from Leading Thinkers on Positive Organizations* (San Francisco: Berrett-Koehler, 2014), Page xiii.

16 Ibid., Pages 2–3.

17 Bob Tewksbury and Scott Miller, *Ninety Percent Mental: An All-Star Player Turned Mental Skills Coach Reveals the Hidden Game of Baseball* (New York: Hatchette Books, 2018), Page 132.

18 Dutton and Spreitzer, *How to Be a Positive Leader*, Pages 45–54.

19 Quoted in His Holiness the Dalai Lama, Archbishop Desmond Tutu, and Douglas Abrams, *The Book of Joy: Lasting Happiness in a Changing World* (New York: Penguin House, 2016), Page 49.

20 John Tierney and Roy F. Baumeister, *The Power of Bad: How the Negativity Effect Rules Us and How We Can Control It* (New York: Penguin Press, 2019), Pages 27, 58 and 70–71.

21 Kim Cameron, "Positive Leadership" Executive Education Class (University of Michigan, Ann Arbor, MI, December 2017).

22 Kim Cameron, "Positive Links" presentation by Ryan Quinn (University of Michigan, Ann Arbor, MI, February 2016).

23 Tierney and Baumeister, *The Power of Bad*, Pages 25–27.

24 Gladwell, *Blink*, Pages 52–55.

25 Ibid., Page 56.

26 Ibid., Pages 56–58.

27 Daniel Lerner and Alan Schlechter, MD, *U Thrive: How to Succeed in College and Life* (New York: Little Brown Spark, 2017), Page 27.

28 Bob Harig, "Jordan Speith Shoots Quadruple-Bogey on 12th Hole at the Masters," *ESPN*, April 10, 2016, https://www.espn.com/golf/story/_/id/15178079/2016-masters-jordan-spieth-shoots-quadruple-bogey-12th-hole

29 Ewan Murray, "Jordan Speith's Astonishing 13th-hole Recovery Paves Way for Open Victory," *The Guardian*, July 23, 2017, https://www.theguardian.com/sport/2017/jul/23/the-open-2017-jordan-spieth

30 Tewksbury and Miller, *Ninety Percent Mental*, Page 132.

31 Lerner and Schlechter, MD, *U Thrive*, Pages 16–17.

32 Ibid., Page 17.

33 Michelle Seger, *No Sweat: How the Simple Science of Motivation Can Bring You a Lifetime of Fitness* (New York: Amacom, 2015), Pages 159–160.

34 Lerner and Schlechter, MD, *U Thrive*, Pages 20, 28.

35 Gretchen Spreitzer, "Positive Leadership" Executive Education Class (University of Michigan, Ann Arbor, MI, December 2017).

36 Christopher White, "YPO Presentation" (University of Michigan, Ann Arbor, MI, November 2018).

37 Lerner and Schlechter, MD, *U Thrive*, Page 63.

38 Simon Sinek, *Leaders Eat Last: Why Some Teams Pull Together and Others Don't* (New York: Penguin Random House, 2017), Pages 47–64.

39 Ibid., Pages 87–88.

40 Daniel Coyle, *The Culture Code: The Secrets of Highly Successful Groups* (New York: Bantam Books, 2018), Page 24.

41 Shirli Kopelman, "Positive Leadership" Executive Education Class (University of Michigan, Ann Arbor, MI, December 2017).

42 Lerner and Schlechter, MD, *U Thrive*, Page 19.

43 Ibid., Pages 81–83.

44 Michelle McQuaid, "Presentation to the Center for Positive Organizations" (University of Michigan Zoom link, May 2020).

45 Lerner and Schlechter, MD, *U Thrive*, Page 83.

46 Michelle McQuaid, "Presentation to the Center for Positive Organizations" (University of Michigan Zoom link, May 2020).

47 Lerner and Schlechter, MD, *U Thrive*, Page 83.

48 Michelle McQuaid, "Presentation to the Center for Positive Organizations" (University of Michigan Zoom link, May 2020).

49 Roger Newton, Telephone interview with the author, May 2020.

50 Ryan Quinn, "Positive Links" presentation (University of Michigan, Ann Arbor, MI, February 2016).

51 Ibid.

52 Lindy Greer, "Positive Links" presentation (University of Michigan, Ann Arbor, MI, February 2020).

53 Ryan Quinn, "Positive Links" presentation (University of Michigan, Ann Arbor, MI, February 2016).

54 Rob Murphy, *Deep: Alive with Purpose* (United States: Open Gates Entertainment & Sports, 2019), Page 204.

55 Ibid., Page 118.

56 Tewksbury and Miller, *Ninety Percent Mental,* Page 13.

57 Gretchen Spreitzer and Christine Porath, "Creating Sustainable Performance," *Harvard Business Review,* January—February, 2012: Reprint R1201F.

58 Peggy Anderson, *Great Quotes from Great Leaders: Words from the Leaders Who Shaped the World* (Naperville: Simple Truths, 2017), Page 270.

59 Victor Strecher, *Life on Purpose: How Living for What Matters Most Changes Everything* (New York: Harper One, 2016).

60 Blake E. Ashforth, Spencer H. Harrison, and Kevin G. Corley, "Identification in Organizations: An Examination of Four Fundamental Questions" *Journal of Management,* March 2008, https://www.researchgate .net/publication/234021306_Identification_in_Organizations_An _Examination_of_Four_Fundamental_Questions

61 Ryan W. Quinn and Robert E. Quinn, *Lift: The Fundamental State of Leadership* (Oakland: Berrett-Koehler, 2015), Page 21.

62 Adam Grant, *Give and Take: Why Helping Others Drives Our Success* (New York: Penguin Books, 2013), Page 63.

63 Quinn and Quinn, *Lift,* Pages 99–133.

64 Sonenshein, *Stretch,* Page 220.

65 Strecher, *Life on Purpose,* Page 40.

66 Michelle Seger, *No Sweat,* Page 187.

67 Cameron, *Practicing Positive Leadership,* Page 65.

68 Baker, *All You Have to Do Is Ask,* Pages 70–71.

69 Ibid., Pages 61–62.

70 Ibid., Pages 65–70.

71 Lerner and Schlechter, MD, *U Thrive,* Pages 126–127.

72 Ibid., Pages 123–124.

73 Michelle Seger, *No Sweat,* Pages 28–29.

74 Duhigg, *The Power of Habit,* Pages 141–144.

75 Ibid., Pages 149–150.

76 Robert B. Cialdini, *Influence* (New York: Harper Collins, 2009), Page 115.

77 Duhigg, *The Power of Habit,* Pages 17–20, 47–51, 78–85.

78 Lerner and Schlechter, MD, *U Thrive,* Pages 167, 227.

79 Sheryl Sandberg and Adam Grant, *Option B: Facing Adversity, Building Resilience, and Finding Joy* (New York: Alfred A. Knopf, 2017), Page 16.

80 Ibid., Page 111.

81 Karen Reivich and Andrew Schatte, *The Resilience Factor: 7 Keys to Finding Your Inner Strength and Overcoming Life's Hurdles* (New York: Three Rivers Press, 2002), Location 1033.

82 Reivich and Schatte, *The Resilience Factor,* Location 1528–2416.

83 Sandberg and Grant, *Option B,* Page 18.

84 Ibid., Page 21.

85 Reivich and Schatte, *The Resilience Factor,* Location 514.

86 Ibid., *The Resilience Factor.*

87 Olivia Fox Cobane, *The Charisma Myth: How Anyone Can Master the Art and Science of Personal Magnetism* (New York: Portfolio/Penguin, 2013), Pages 53–54.

88 Willie Mays and John Shea, *24: Life Stories and Lessons from the Say Hey Kid* (New York: St Martin's Press, 2020), Page 137.

89 Sandberg and Grant, *Option B,* Page 79.

90 Csíkszentmihályi , *Flow,* Page 64.

91 Reivich and Schatte, *The Resilience Factor,* Location 912.

92 Angela Duckworth, *Grit: The Power and Passion of Perseverance* (New York: Scribner, 2018), Pages 41–43.

93 Robert Vallerand, "Positive Links" presentation (University of Michigan, Ann Arbor, MI, September 2018).

94 Edward L. Deci and Richard Flaste, *Why We Do What We Do: Understanding Self-Motivation* (New York: Penguin Group, 1995), Pages 97–98.

95 Ibid.

96 Ibid., Pages 57–73.

97 Bradley Staats, *Never Stop Learning: Stay Relevant, Reinvent Yourself, and Thrive* (Boston: Harvard Business Review Press, 2018), Pages 81–85.

98 Deci and Flaste, *Why We Do What We Do*, Pages 6–9, 30–43.

99 Duckworth, *Grit*, Pages 171–175.

100 David Cooperrider, "Positive Links" presentation (University of Michigan, Ann Arbor, MI, April 2017).

101 Deci and Flaste, *Why We Do What We Do*, Pages 149–155.

102 Ibid., Pages 88–90.

103 Csíkszentmihályi, *Flow*, Page 88.

104 Deci and Flaste, *Why We Do What We Do*, Pages 2–4, 176.

105 Michael Puett and Christine Gross-Loh, *The Path: What Chinese Philosophers Can Teach Us about the Good Life* (New York: Thorndike Press, 2016), Page 101–109.

106 Csíkszentmihályi, *Flow*, Page 65.

107 Michelle Seger, *No Sweat*, Pages 46–47.

108 Csíkszentmihályi, *Flow*, Pages 49–70.

109 Dutton, and Spreitzer, *How to be a Positive Leader*, Page 47.

110 Lerner and Schlechter, MD, *U Thrive*, Page 63.

111 Don Barden, Presentation at the Conference on Business and Poverty (Oxford University, Oxford England, July 2016).

112 Mitch Albom, "Even the Experts Were Wrong," *Detroit Free Press*, February 3, 2019.

113 Bill Pennington, "Hidden Gems: Do the Patriots Find Them or Create Them?" *The New York Times*, February 2, 2019.

114 Cobane, *The Charisma Myth*, Pages 98–114.

115 Michelle Obama, *Becoming* (New York: Crown Publishing Group, 2018), Page 152.

116 Cobane, *The Charisma Myth*, Pages 98–114.

117 Daniel Pink, *To Sell Is Human: The Surprising Truth about Moving Others* (New York: Riverhead Books, 2012), Page 70.

118 Gretchen Spreitzer and Christine Porath, "Creating Sustainable Performance," *Harvard Business Review*, January – February, 2012: Reprint R1201F.

119 Robert Emmons, "Three Surprising Ways That Gratitude Works at Work" *Workplace*, Greater Good Science Center, October 11, 2017, https://greatergood.berkeley.edu/article/item/three_surprising_ways_that _gratitude_works_at_work

120 Strecher, *Life on Purpose*, Pages 132–134.

121 Lerner and Schlechter, MD, *U Thrive*, Page 213.

122 Arianna Huffington, *The Sleep Revolution: Transforming Your Life One Night at a Time* (New York: Harmony Books, 2016), Page 41.

123 Daniel Pink, *When: The Scientific Secrets of Perfect Timing* (New York: Riverhead Books, 2018), Pages 66–69.

124 Strecher, *Life on Purpose*, Pages 131–142.

125 Huffington, *The Sleep Revolution*, Pages 212–214.

126 Strecher, *Life on Purpose*, Pages 201–216.

127 David Robson, "The Ingredients for a Longer Life," *100 Year Life / Health bbc.com Features Newsletter*, May 12, 2020, https://www.bbc.com/future /article/20200512-the-ingredients-that-hold-the-secret-to-a-long-life

128 Michelle Seger, *No Sweat*, Pages 12, 17–28, 87–95, 104–106.

129 Ibid., Pages 38–41.

130 Atul Gawande, *Being Mortal: Medicine and What Matters Most* (New York: Metropolitan Books, 2014), Pages 94–98.

131 Grant, *Give and Take*, Pages 247.

132 Strecher, *Life on Purpose*, Page 230.

133 John Carreyrou, *Bad Blood: Secrets and Lies in a Silicon Valley Startup* (New York: Vintage Books, 2020), and John Carreyrou, "Theranos Whisleblower Shook the Company—and His Family," *Wall Street Journal*, November 18, 2016.

134 Sara Randazzo, Heather Somerville, and Christopher Weaver, "The Elizabeth Holmes Verdict: Theranos Founder is Guilty on Four of 11 Charges in Fraud Trial," *Wall Street Journal*, January 3, 2022.

135 Lao Tzu, "Small Spaces (Small Spaces, #1) by Katherine Arden." Goodreads. Accessed March 23, 2022. https://www.goodreads.com/en/book /show/36959639-small-spaces

136 "Woodrow Wilson Quote." AZ Quotes. Accessed March 23, 2022. https ://www.azquotes.com/quote/765428

137 Strecher, *Life on Purpose*, Page 11.

138 Strecher, *Life on Purpose*.

139 "Two Most Important Days in Your Life: The Day You Were Born and the Day You Discover Why." Quote Investigator, November 21, 2020. https ://quoteinvestigator.com/2016/06/22/why/

140 Robert E. Quinn, "+ Lab" presentation (Center for Positive Organizations, University of Michigan, Ann Arbor, MI, November 2017).

141 Strecher, *Life on Purpose*, Pages 13–16.

142 Ibid., Pages 16–17.

143 Pink, *When*, Page 216.

144 Bruce N. Pfau, "What Do Millenials Really Want at Work? The Same Things the Rest of Us Do," *Harvard Business Review*, April 7, 2016, https://hbr.org /2016/04/what-do-millennials-really-want-at-work; Bruce N. Pfau, (Main Session, Positive Business Conference, Ann Arbor, MI, May 2016).

145 David Woods, "Two Thirds of Staff Would Go the Extra Mile for an Organization with a 'Purpose' Beyond Commercial Gain, Survey of 4,000 Shows," *HR Magazine*, May 23, 2012, https://www.hrmagazine.co.uk /content/other/two-thirds-of-staff-would-go-the-extra-mile-for-an -organisation-with-a-purpose-beyond-commercial-gain-survey-of-4-000-shows

146 Cliff Zukin and Mark Szeltner, "Talent Report: What Workers Want in 2012," *Net Impact*, May, 2012, https://netimpact.org/sites/default/files /documents/what-workers-want-2012-summary.pdf

147 Charlotte Alter, Suyin Haynes, and Justin Worland, "Time: 2019 Person of the Year—Greta Thurnberg," *Time*, December 23, 2019, https://time.com /person-of-the-year-2019-greta-thunberg/

148 Duckworth, *Grit*, Pages 143–144.

149 Matthew Forti, Commencement Speech, Northwestern University (Ryan Field, Evanston, IL, June 2017) and https://en.wikipedia.org/wiki/One _Acre_Fund

150 Larry Brilliant, Commencement Speech - University of Michigan Medical School (Hill Auditorium, Ann Arbor, MI, May 2014) and https://en .wikipedia.org/wiki/Larry_Brilliant

151 Sandberg and Grant, *Option B*, Page 67.

152 David McCullough, *The Wright Brothers* (New York: Simon & Schuster, 2016).

153 Robert E. Quinn, Katherine Heynoski, Mike Thomas, and Gretchen M. Spreitzer, *The Best Teacher in You: How to Accelerate Learning and Change Lives* (San Francisco: Berrett-Koehler, 2014), Pages 9–15.

154 Sonenshein, *Stretch*, Pages 127–130.

155 Coyle, *The Culture Code*, Page 187.

156 Kim Cameron, "Positive Leadership" Executive Education Class (University of Michigan, Ann Arbor, MI, December 2017)

157 Ibid.

158 Geri Stengel, "Could the Next Steve Jobs Be a Black Woman? Not If She Only Gets Funding Crumbs," *Women Forbes*, May 3, 2017; Sequoia Blodgett, "Wealthlife CEO Angel Rich Teaches You Finance Through Gamification," *Black Enterprise*, August 25, 2017; Kelly D. Evans, "Meet Angel Rich, the Entrepreneur Whose App Tackles Financial Literacy for Youth," *The Undefeated*, September 18, 2017.

159 Dutton and Spreitzer, with Oana Branzei, *How to be a Positive Leader,* Page 116.

160 Strecher, *Life on Purpose*, Pages 221–227.

161 Lopez Lomong and Mark Tabb, *Running for My Life: One Lost Boy's Journey from the Killing Fields of Sudan to the Olympic Games* (Nashville: Nelson Books, 2016).

162 Patricia Albere, *The Evolutionary Collective*, https://evolutionarycollective .com/blogposts/tied-together-in-the-single-garment-of-destiny/

163 Robert E. Quinn, "+ Lab" presentation (Center for Positive Organizations, University of Michigan, Ann Arbor, MI, November 2017).

164 Puett and Gross-Loh, *The Path*, Page 35.

165 Ibid., Page 43–51.

166 Ibid., *The Path*, Page 11–14.

167 Don Barden, Presentation at the Conference on Business and Poverty (Oxford University, Oxford England, July 2016).

168 His Holiness the Dalai Lama, Archbishop Desmond Tutu and Douglas Abrams, *The Book of Joy*, Pages 43–44.

169 Thomas J. Sugrue, *Origins of the Urban Crisis: Race and Inequality in Postwar Detroit* (Princeton: Princeton University Press, 2014) and https://www.michiganradio.org/families-community/2017-07-17/historian-divide-between-white-detroit-and-black-detroit-led-to-citys-1967-rebellion

170 Lori Laken Hutcherson, "My White Friend Asked Me on Facebook to Explain White Privilege. I Decided to be Honest.," *Yes! Magazine*, September 8, 2017.

171 Jane E. Dutton, *Energize Your Workplace: How to Create and Sustain High-Quality Connections at Work,* (San Francisco: Jossey-Bass, 2003), Page 37.

172 Richard Branson, *The Virgin Way: Everything I Know About Leadership* (New York: Portfolio/Penguin, 2014), Pages 29–51.

173 Branson, *The Virgin Way*, Pages 40–42, 51.

174 Dutton, *Energize Your Workplace,* Page 39.

175 Branson, *The Virgin Way*, Page 32.

176 Grant, *Give and Take*, Page 264.

177 Baker, *All You Have to Do Is Ask,* Page 18.

178 Lerner and Schlechter, MD, *U Thrive*, Pages 46–54.

179 Coyle, *The Culture Code*, Page 36–38.

180 Cameron, *Practicing Positive Leadership,* Page 32.

181 Robert E. Quinn, "From Knowing to Learning: The Power of Question-Storming," *Robert E. Quinn Blog*, May 1, 2020.

182 David Robson, *The Intelligence Trap: Why Smart People Make Dumb Mistakes* (New York: W.W. Norton & Company, 2021); blog post, @d_a_robson on Twitter.

183 Coyle, *The Culture Code*, Page 23.

184 Gratitude and Well Being Work Conference Initation, *Greater Good Science Center*, November 17, 2017.

185 Robert Emmons, in Vishen Lakhiani, *Code of the Extraordinary Mind: 10 Uncoventional Laws to Redefine Your Life & Succeed on Your Own Terms* (Emmaus/New York: Rodale, 2020), Page 134.

186 Blair and Rita Justice, "Grateful-ology: The Science and Research of Gratitude," *Wellbeing*, November 20, 2011, https://www.kindredmedia.org/2011/11/grateful-ology-the-science-and-research-of-gratitude/

187 Don Barden, Presentation at the Conference on Business and Poverty (Oxford University, Oxford England, July 2016).

188 Grant, *Give and Take,* Pages 43–44.

189 Brené Brown, *Braving the Wilderness: The Quest for True Belonging and the Courage to Stand Alone* (New York: Random House, 2019), Page 147.

190   Kim Cameron, "Positive Leadership" Executive Education Class (University of Michigan, Ann Arbor, MI, December 2017).

191   Sandberg and Grant, *Option B,* Page 18; Lerner and Schlechter, *U Thrive,* Page 269; Kim Cameron, *Positive Leadership: Strategies for Extraordinary Performance* (San Francisco: Berrett-Koehler, 2012).

192   Lerner and Schlechter, *U Thrive,* Page 29.

193   Rich Smalling, *Practically Positive: Practices for Creating a Thriving Organization* (Austin: Per Capita Publishing, 2021), Pages 126–127.

194   Sandberg and Grant, *Option B,* Page 83.

195   Coyle, *The Culture Code,* Page 79.

196   Jim Kalb, "Unconventional Motivation," *Optifuse Blog,* August 16, 2013.

197   Jimmy Carter, *A Full Life: Reflections at Ninety* (New York: Simon & Schuster, 2016), Pages 154–156.

198   David Cooperrider, "Positive Links" presentation (University of Michigan, Ann Arbor, MI, April 2017).

199   David Cooperrider, Diana Whitney and Jacqueline M. Stavros, *Appreciative Inquiry Handbook: For Leaders of Change* (Brunswick / San Francisco: Crown Custom Publishing / Berrett-Koehler, 2008.

200   Simon Sinek, *Start with Why: How Great Leaders Inspire Everyone to Take Action* (New York: Portfolio/Penguin, 2011), Pages 37–65.

201   Sergio Caredda, "Models: The Lippitt-Knoster Model for Managing Complex Change," *sergiocaredda.eu,* https://sergiocaredda.eu/organisation/tools/models-the-lippitt-knoster-model-for-managing-complex-change/

202   Gary Harvey, conversation with author, circa 2008.

203   Robert E. Quinn, conversation with author, circa 2017.

204   Grant, *Give and Take,* Pages 252–258.

205   Quinn, *Deep Change,* Page 65.

206   Gerald F. Davis, *Managed by Markets: How Finance Reshaped America* (Oxford, England: Oxford University Press, 2011).

207   Quinn, *Deep Change,* Page 168.

208   Richard Beckhard and Reuben Harris, *Organizational Transitions: Managing Complex Change* (Reading: Addison-Wesley, 1998).

209   Sonenshein, *Stretch,* Pages 201–203.

210   Baker, *All You Have To Do Is Ask,* Page 72.

211   Ibid., Pages 5–7.

212   Ibid., Page 81.

213   Dutton and Spreitzer, with Scott Sonenshein, *How to be a Positive Leader,* Pages 141–142.

214   Pink, *When,* Page 218.

215   Ibid., Pages 25, 140 and 153.

216   Lerner and Schlechter, *U Thrive,* Page 112; Coyle, *The Culture Code,* Page 181.

217 Jeff Stibel, former vice chairman, Dun & Bradstreet, April 16, 2018, https://www.dnb.com/perspectives/small-business/failure-wall-encouraging-culture-success.html

218 Shirli Kopelman, "Positive Leadership" Executive Education Class (University of Michigan, Ann Arbor, MI, December 2017).

219 Puett and Gross-Loh, *The Path*, Page 71.

220 Cameron, *Positive Leadership*, Pages 55–56.

221 Wayne Baker, Presentation to the Consortium of the Center for Positive Organizations (Ann Arbor, MI, November 2016).

222 Ibid.

223 Dutton and Spreitzer, with Robert E. Quinn and Anjan V. Thakor, *How to be a Positive Leader*, Page 102.

224 Cameron, *Practicing Positive Leadership*, Pages 29, 37.

225 Sandberg and Grant, *Option B*, Page 133.

226 Dutton, *Energize Your Workplace*, Pages 164–166.

227 Confucious, "Confucius Quotes." BrainyQuote. Xplore. Accessed March 23, 2022. https://www.brainyquote.com/quotes/confucius_136802

228 Simon Sinek, *Start with Why*, Page 158; Cameron, *Practicing Positive Leadership*, Pages 34–37.

229 Cameron, *Practicing Positive Leadership*, Pages 28–36.

230 Presentation at the Conference on Business and Poverty (Oxford University, Oxford England, July 2016).

231 Presentation at the Positive Business Conference (University of Michigan, Ann Arbor, MI, May 2019).

232 Jack Stack and Bo Burlingame, *The Great Game of Business: The Only Sensible Way to Run a Company* (London: Profile Books, 2014); Cameron, *Practicing Positive Leadership*, Pages 43–44.

233 Cameron, *Practicing Positive Leadership*, Page 45.

234 Richard Sheridan, *Joy, Inc.: How We Built a Workplace People Love* (New York: Penguin/Portfolio, 2015), Pages 124 and 129.

235 Stack and Burlingame, *The Great Game of Business*, Pages 87–125; Spreitzer and Porath, "Creating Sustainable Performance."

236 Gerald F. Davis and Christopher J. White, *Changing Your Company From the Inside Out* (Boston: Harvard Business Review Press, 2015).

237 Sonenshein, *Stretch*, Pages 184–188.

238 Dutton and Spreitzer, with Scott Sonenshein, *How to Be a Positive Leader*, Pages 136–146.

239 Baker, *All You Have to Do Is Ask*, Pages 83–85.

240 Peggy Anderson, *Great Quotes from Great Leaders*, Page 288.

241 Foster Cline and Jim Fay, *Parenting with Love and Logic: Teaching Children Responsibility* (Colorado: Picton Press, 2006)

242 Dutton, *Energize Your Workplace*, Pages 1–20.

243 Jane Dutton, "Positive Leadership" Executive Education Class (University of Michigan, Ann Arbor, MI, December 2017).

244 Baker, *All You Have to Do Is Ask,* Page 93.

245 Dutton, *Energize Your Workplace,* Pages 37–39, 81–85.

246 Gretchen Spreitzer, Presentation to the Center for Positive Organizations (University of Michigan, Ann Arbor, MI, November 2018).

247 Coyle, *The Culture Code*, Page 127.

248 Dutton, *Energize Your Workplace,* Pages 16–17.

249 Baker, *All You Have to Do Is Ask,* Pages 150.

250 Donald W. Barden, *The Perfect Plan: The Story That Reveals the Secret of the World's Elite Sales and Marketing Teams* (Bloomington: Westbow Press, 2012), Location 592–620.

251 Suzanne Segal, Positive Organizational Scholarship Research Conference (University of Michigan, Ann Arbor, MI, June 2019).

252 Dutton, *Energize Your Workplace,* Page 28.

253 Coyle, *The Culture Code*, Pages 36–38; Dutton and Spreitzer, with Lynn Perry Wooten and Erika Hayes James, *How to be a Positive Leader,* Pages 149–151 and 165–166.

254 Dutton, *Energize Your Workplace,* Pages 11–20.

255 Baker, *All You Have to Do Is Ask,* Pages 18.

256 Doris Kearns Goodwin, master class lecture.

257 Dutton, *Energize Your Workplace,* Pages 81–85.

258 Cameron, *Practicing Positive Leadership,* Page 45.

259 Gretchen Spreitzer, Presentation at the Positive Business Conference.

260 Dutton, *Energize Your Workplace,* Page 95.

261 Grant, *Give and Take,* Page 198; Dutton, *Energize Your Workplace,* Pages 60–63, 87–98.

262 Gen. David Perkins, Commander, US Army Doctrine Command, "Positive Links" presentation (University of Michigan, Ann Arbor, MI, November 2016).

263 Monica C. Worline and Jane E. Dutton, *Awakening Compassion at Work: The Quiet Power That Elevates People and Organizations* (Oakland: Berrett-Koehler, 2017).

264 Sandberg and Grant, *Option B,* Pages 60–62.

265 *The American Heritage College Dictionary* (Boston: Houghton Mifflin, 2007)

266 Susan Cain, *Quiet: The Power of Introverts in a World That Can't Stop Talking* (New York: Broadway Books, 2013), Page 141.

267 Olivia Fox Cobane, *The Charisma Myth*, Page 82.

268 Coyle, *The Culture Code*, Pages 104–106.

269 Jane Brody, "Turning Negative Thinkers into Positive Ones," *New York Times*, April 3, 2017.

270   Barbara L. Fredrickson, *Love 2.0: How Our Supreme Emotion Affects Everything We Feel, Think, Do, and Become* (New York: Hudson Street Press, 2013), Page 104.

271   Ibid., Pages 9, 17.

272   Ibid., Pages 68–72.

273   Strecher, *Life on Purpose*, Page 63.

274   Fredrickson, *Love 2.0*, Page 103.

275   Ari Weinzweig, "Positive Leadership" Executive Education Class (University of Michigan, Ann Arbor, MI, December 2017).

276   Frank "El Jefe" Venegas, Presentation at the Conference on Business and Poverty (Oxford University, Oxford England, July 2016).

277   Dutton, *Energize Your Workplace*, Page 7.

278   Dutton and Spreitzer, with Kim Cameron, *How to Be a Positive Leader*, Page 83; Lakhiani, *Code of the Extraordinary Mind*, Pages 139–143.

279   Venegas, Presentation at the Conference on Business and Poverty.

280   Coyle, *The Culture Code*, Page 56.

281   Jennifer L. Eberhardt, *Biased: Uncovering the Hidden Prejudice That Shapes What we See, Think and Do* (New York: Penguin Books, 2020), Pages 212–213.

282   Cameron, *Practicing Positive Leadership*, Pages 80–94.

283   Ibid.

284   Coyle, *The Culture Code*, Page 87.

285   Ibid., Page 165.

286   Kim Cameron, "Positive Leadership" Executive Education Class (University of Michigan, Ann Arbor, MI, December 2017).

287   Quinn and Quinn, *Lift*, Pages 178–197.

288   Tierney and Baumeister, *The Power of Bad*, Pages 99–100.

289   Coyle, *The Culture Code*, Page 161.

290   Lakhiani, *Code of the Extraordinary Mind*, Page 113.

291   Olivia Fox Cobane, *The Charisma Myth*, Page 14.

292   Gretchen Spreitzer, Presentation to the Center for Positive Organizations of Rubenstein, Meyer, and Evans 2001 research (University of Michigan, Ann Arbor, MI, November 2018).

293   Grant, *Give and Take*, Page 73.

294   Ibid., Page 158.

295   David Herbert Donald, *Lincoln* (London: Jonathan Cape Random House, 1995); Elton Trueblood and Alonzo L. McDonald, *Abraham Lincoln: The Spiritual Growth of a Public Man* (The Trinity Forum); Grant, *Give and Take*, Pages 10–16.

296   David Mayer, Presentation to the Center for Positive Organizations (University of Michigan, via videoconference, October 2017).

297 Christine Porath and Christine Pearson, "The Price of Incivility," *Harvard Business Review*, January–February 2013.

298 Ibid.

299 Cain, *Quiet*, Page 190.

300 Danny Boyle and Aaron Sorkin, *Steve Jobs* (biographical drama), 2015.

301 Coyle, *The Culture Code*, Pages 71–73.

302 Peggy Anderson, *Great Quotes from Great Leaders*, Page 180.

303 Coyle, *The Culture Code*, Pages 48–56.

304 Raul Dominguez, "Spurs' Gregg Popovich Becomes NBA Regular-Season Wins Leader," AP NEWS, Associated Press, March 12, 2022. https://apnews.com/article/san-antonio-spurs-utah-jazz-nba-sports-don-nelson-cc05db4c7ccea579bdde7c1cffae1a19

305 Gabe Polsky, *In Search of Greatness* (documentary), 2018.

306 Roger Newton, telephone interview with the author, May 2020.

307 Staats, *Never Stop Learning*, Page 72; Dutton and Spreitzer, with Scott Sonenshein, *How to be a Positive Leader*, Pages 136–146.

308 Sandberg and Grant, *Option B*, Page 77.

309 Shirli Kopelman, "Positive Leadership" Executive Education Class (University of Michigan, Ann Arbor, MI, December 2017).

310 John Beilein, Telephone interview with the author, May 2020; Jeff Seidel, "24 Hours of Crazy for U-M Basketball Team," *Detroit Free Press*, March 9, 2017; Shawn Windsor, "How Michigan Basketball Plane Crash Changed John Beilein and His Wife," *Detroit Free Press*, May 22, 2017.

311 Charlotte Alter, Suyin Haynes, and Justin Worland, "Time: 2019 Person of the Year."

312 Capt. L. David Marquet, USN (RET), *Turn the Ship Around: A True Story of Turning Followers into Leaders* (New York: Portfolio/Penguin, 2012).

313 Juan Riboldi, *The Path of Ascent: The Five Principles For Mastering Change* (North Providence, RI: Ascent Advisor), 2009.

314 BrainyQuote, https://www.brainyquote.com/authors/neil-armstrong-quotes

315 Gerald F. Davis, *The Vanishing American Corporation: Navigating the Hazards of a New Economy* (Oakland: Berrett-Kohler, 2016); Gerald F. Davis, *Managed by the Markets: How Finance Reshaped America* (Oxford, UK: Oxford University Press), 2009.

316 Gretchen Spreitzer, "Positive Leadership" Executive Education Class; Gretchen Spreitzer Presentation (Main Session, Positive Business Conference, Ann Arbor, MI, May 2019).

317 Davis, *Managed by the Markets*.

318 Cameron, *Practicing Positive Leadership*, Pages 117–122.

319 Kim S. Cameron and Gretchen M Spreitzer, *The Oxford Guide to Positive Organizational Scholarship* (New York: Oxford University Press, 2012), Pages 1029–1032.

320 Cameron, *Practicing Positive Leadership,* Page 120.

321 Grant, *Give and Take*, Page 76.

322 Cameron, *Practicing Positive Leadership,* Page 28.

323 Quinn and Quinn, *Lift*, Pages 178–197.

324 Dutton, *Energize Your Workplace,* Pages 87–88.

325 Reivich and Schatte, *The Resilience Factor*, Location 128.

326 Cameron and Spreitzer, *The Oxford Guide to Postive Organizational Scholarship.*

327 John Quincy Adams, "John Quincy Adams Quotes (Author of Letters of John Quincy Adams to His Son on the Bible and Its Teaching)." Goodreads. Goodreads. Accessed March 23, 2022. https://www.goodreads.com/author/quotes/117066.John_Quincy_Adams

328 Peggy Anderson, *Great Quotes from Great Leaders,* Page 130.